POWER TO
THE DANCERS!

SELF-ACTUALIZATION FOR WOMEN
THROUGH DANCE

WITH WORKSHOPS FOR TEACHERS
AND OTHERS

Beverly Kalinin

Published by

METAMORPHOUS PRESS
P.O. Box 10616
Portland, Oregon 97210

ISBN 0-943920-44-2

Typography and Design by Cy-Ann Designs, Portland, Oregon

Printed in U.S.A.

DEDICATION

This book is dedicated with love
to my dancing friends
and especially to

Zachary "I can dance, you can dance" Zakon
Sweet Sue Glazer, Queen of New Orleans Jazz
Leonore Alaniz, Weaver of Dance Designs
Moon Jude Pruett, Sky Dancer
Susie Star Laughton, alias Dancing Mountain
Isadora Duncan, dancing invisible in the wind

and
most lovingly to

Beboka Bob Kalinin, who would rather be fishing.

Photo: Linda Wimsey

. . . woman dips to golden power,
her center, source of silken strength
where confidence like coral gathers
with creativity, her pearl;
and lifting, enriched, she extends
then towards the flow . . .

TABLE OF CONTENTS

Foreword xi

PART I 1

"From this third-story window my eyes
dance across wires . . ." 3

Linda at the Supermarket 5

"I remember beginning to dance . . ." 6

"1939. The sibling was born." 6

"Attending polished performances turns me off." 6

"I learned to jitterbug in 1947 . . ." 7

Reincarnation 9

The Bricker Brothers: A Mini Melodrama 10

"Jefferson Dance Band's exchange show . . ." 14

1950. The Dark Age 14

1959. Satori via Dance 15

Wonder Woman 16

Body Expectations, And Lack Of 17

Damn Black Man 18

I Can Dance; You Can Dance 18

Friday Afternoons 1972 19

"Audition." 20

Splintered 22

Berkeley Dance Party 23

Dancing Alone 24

"I nearly always dance barefooted." 25

bare feet dancing 26

Sunday Salon   26
Dance Truths   28
"When I have danced the night before . . ."   29
I *am* the Music   29
Meditation   32
Down Day   33
The Psychology of Flow   33
"I am partner to powerful Wind . . ."   37
Off Center with Ballet   38
"Soul versus technique."   39
Let's Boogie, 1975   40
"You sure love teaching . . ."   41
Eleanor in Class   41
Improvisation   43
Creative Dance and Evolution   44
Ego and Id   45
Correlations   46
"A metaphor, a dream . . ."   46
Doing vs. Teaching   48

PART II
Improvisational Rock Dance Workshops   53
    Workshop I   55
    Workshop II   70
    Workshop III   84
    Workshop IV   99
A Final Thought Regarding the Improvi-
sational Rock Dance Workshops   110

Creative Dance Workshops   121
    I Improvisation   123
    II The Physical Tools   128

Creative Dance Workshops *Continued*

III With Others   131
IV Sounds   136
V Interpretations   139
VI Holistic Dance   143

Dance Yoga-Cize   151

Music Index
Music for Improvisational Rock Dance
Workshops   159
   Workshop I   159
   Workshop II   160
   Workshop III   162
   Workshop IV   163

Music for Creative Dance Workshops   164

Music for Dance Yoga-Cize   166

A Note on The Music List   169

FOREWORD

The idea that dancing could be a vehicle for women for actualizing their powerful selves originally occurred to me when I discovered that dance kept reappearing at crucial times through the history of my personal growth and when I began meeting so many women who desperately wanted to dance.

I realized that dancing, this marvelous tool, had served throughout my life as an opening device with which I probed for my hidden self power, drew it forth, nurtured its development and increasing strength through the years, and finally claimed it for an integral part of my true self.

How had dancing helped me live more fully, I wondered? Why are other women drawn to dance as to a kindred soul who will nurture and support them in hard times? What does dancing do for us?

The answer, reduced to its simplest form, is that dance is movement and movement is life. Whether our dance movement is relaxation, meditation, exercise, or communication, it *flows*, as does life, bringing us from one point to the next in our journeys. In the flowing process we satisfy our natural urge to respond to all of life's rhythms.

When I began teaching dance seven years ago I met women who had yearned to dance all their lives. They did not seek to be professional performers; they wanted simply to move comfortably in social dancing. They needed more than ballroom dancing with its prescribed steps. (They would not have enrolled in my classes if this were not so.) They wanted to express themselves through their bodies. They wanted to move easily. They desired to feel free. They craved self-confidence — not only in dancing.

I decided I must use dance in my classes as the powerful tool that had accompanied *my* development. I suspected that the personal histories of the students were colored by sporadic dancing experiences similar to my own. I felt that if other women could trace dance through their lives, as I have done in Part I of *Power To The Dancers!*, they would recognize its special worth as growth's guide. At the very least each woman would appreciate the design interwoven throughout her life by dance.

So, Part I presents chronologically dated entries of lifelong dancing experiences with which, I hope, the reader will identify. The entries consist of essays, poems, historical anecdotes, dreams, observations about dancing and teaching, and even a mini melodrama.

Part II is for women who teach others to dance and for women who teach themselves. The Improvisational Rock Dance Workshops, the Creative Dance Classes, and Dance Yoga-Cize comprise Part II, including a complete Music Index.

Often I have been asked if men can profit from this book. Of course men can achieve personal growth through dancing! Historically, dance has not been sanctioned for men in the American culture. Young boys are denied dancing and older ones are discouraged from expressing themselves through movement other than sports. As a result, men not only have been denied a valuable outlet

xii

through which they may acknowledge and express feelings, but both sexes have been deprived of a wonderful way of better understanding each other. Furthermore, far fewer men than women use dance for self-exploration and for developing a higher world consciousness. Shared dancing experiences for me, therefore, have occurred mostly with women companions. For this reason — and because I want women to feel they are just as important as men are and I do not think they do — I have chosen to emphasize women's rather than men's personal growth through dance.

Finally, in writing this book I entice those women to open themselves who love to dance, who teach others, who feel movement's power, and who desire to explore dancing as a catalyst for personal growth.

PART I

ESSAYS
POEMS
HISTORICAL ANECDOTES
DREAMS
OBSERVATIONS ON TEACHING

Part One

From this third-story window my eyes dance across wires — fragile multi-stranded ones dipping gently with grace; steady symmetrical electrical bus wires dependably parallel; stable fat cables; taut telephone wires emanating as from one center, then separating and catapulting through space, filling the sky with angles, and trembling slightly. A cold gusty wind enhances their dance.

My eyes continue to flow, up a telephone pole, past the pattern of conduits and connections near the top, past the seagull at the tip to the clear blue sky, and soar beyond. From one swaying wire to the next I swing as on a trapeze; I fly as in a dream. In slow motion I swim through air, twisting, stretching, catching a wire, flowing, lifting, supported as by water, a mermaid gliding, powerized by solar energy and dance.

I flash on an old recurring dream where I dance from table to chair to steps and other raised surfaces, never the floor. I leap lightly, lingering in air, touching down easily only to rise up again forcefully. The dream began in the powerless days of my childhood. (Only with the emergence of adult self-actualization had the frequency of this dream diminished steadily.)

Little girls of my generation were influenced by 1940 movie musicals where we flew with Gene Kelly from one pedestal to the next through the magic land of stage dance. Because I was impressionable and loved dance movement, as many other little girls did, I relived all those musicals in my basement, a spacious San Francisco garage of cozy nooks and crannies, dark and secret. I strung a blanket on a clothesline and set up assorted seats for an audience of younger neighborhood children. On lonely days I performed for myself, as in adult years I learned to appreciate the act of dancing alone, nurturing myself with the movements instead of nourishing onlookers and waiting for them to feed me back.

I began to dance earlier, even, than the days of the 1940 basement spectaculars. As my body became strengthened with spoonfuls of cod liver oil ministered by my mother, so did my spirit thrive on dollops of dance consumed throughout childhood. I have no memory of my toddler self bouncing and swaying to music, as each of us did. When I see a baby dance I am excited that her total being — chubby body, shiny eyes, little soul — is an expression of the innate rhythm each of us brings to life, helped by mother during those nine months when she provided us initially with space, fluid, and tempo in which to expand. I want to shout to the baby's mother, "don't cause her to stop," just as I entreat my adult dance students to recapture the natural rhythm of childhood.

At different ages and for various reasons we stop our flow of movement. A part of our soul begins to atrophy when our natural energy becomes narrowed, channeled, reduced, and at times extinguished like the flicker of a candle, when that flame could go on burning for a lifetime. Happily, many candles become relighted. My dance flame never went out altogether but it burned weakly at times, as it does for many women, nearly drowning in the collection of melted wax for which there seemed no outlet.

* * *

I saw Linda in the supermarket today, though I could not remember her name or where I had known her. From one of my Improvisational Rock Workshops she said. Oh yes, and a slim leotarded body in black slipped past me, lady-like, looking right, her dance demure and dainty. We stood in the aisle and talked dance. Her eyes were large and very round, the lashes evenly spaced and stiff with mascara. At first I only glanced at her, then down the aisle, to her cart, looping back to her circle eyes. She sought a dance class. My mouth told her of my new one while my mind remembered milk and eggs.

Then, like a distress alert, the eyes widened, her mouth fired faster. The surrounding blur of foodstuffs fell away, as, hypnotized, I saw only those painful dark eyes. "I have got to dance," she implored. "People think I'm just not grown up or something." I saw piercing anxieties behind her sentences, between her lashes. *Please give me permission to dance*, flashed unspoken. *Please see my human need to create, to express.*

By then I was in her eyes fully. Fluid they were as if by plan preparing to guide her through a gushing escape, allowing her essence to pour forth and flood the space, then rise up, expand, and grow.

Let go, let go, I wanted to scream! Like the boy at the dike, she maintained in abeyance. But she had revealed to me her urgent need to expand. I appreciated the delicate gift. Her parting words were intense. "If you have dance in you, you've got to do it! You're like that aren't you?" Feeling sad and drained I realized how many Lindas there are of us.

* * *

I remember beginning to dance before I was three, tap and acrobatics, the order of the day for little girls then. Lessons at the Betty May Studio on Mission Street in San Francisco. Students needed to be at least three years old but my mother said the woman liked me and made an exception. I do not recall very much. I keep hearing other women say this about their childhoods and I question why we hide so much from ourselves. For me, fleeting positive recollections are mostly connected with dance. Glimpses: Shiny patent leather bows down the front of my costume, bare legs, black shoes tapping to "Annie Doesn't Live Here Anymore," choreographed Shirley Temple gestures, being first in line onto the stage. Once, a yellow-hooded chicken costume with a satin beak. My mother always said I was wonderful. These were the rewarding moments of my young life, just as now dance is a catalyst for my self expression. Some of us women are opening the soft wall of wax, experiencing the flow, and breathing in healthy wafts of movement that rekindle the flame.

* * *

1939. The sibling was born. A boy-child. I was four and a half. Lessons stopped. Dance stopped. Went underground. Damn! I forgive you, Mom.

* * *

Attending polished performances turns me off. A dance troupe's robot-like flawlessness makes spaces between us filled with dreams past, lonely longing, and the lesson of aspiration learned too late.

When I watch I have no body, just saucer-sized eyes. As I leave, my bulk doubles, my legs shrink to stumps, a numb waddling hippo. I wait for my brain to recoup from this trauma to send tender messages of coddled remembrance: that watching is like a verb, action vicariously driven from the past or into the future. That doing is like a noun, a centered entity, a thing, a person, an existential happening. *We can dance now.*

When I pass through the door, I am finally as normal as before I entered the other's reality, allowing her dance values to influence mine.

* * *

I learned to jitterbug in 1947 when I was twelve. We lived in four funky rooms behind our mama-papa grocery store at Page and Laguna in the City — my parents, my brother, and I. Except for the kitchen, the rooms were interchangeable — now a bedroom, then a living room — with either a door or a window or both connecting one room to the next in the manner of Victorian extravagance and Alice-in-Wonderland confusion. For protection, on the sidewalk window, an iron grill that only nurtured my gray-fog fear of the unknown. The front door was in the room my brother and I shared, an old three foot two-by-four jammed under the knob for security. No one used that door. We entered and exited, instead, through the kitchen, down the three narrow dark stairs to the store's crowded back room, around the counter (behind which was hidden in post-war scarcity coveted Dubble Bubble Gum for special customers), and through the little store's belled front door.

Up to that age I remember myself as a timid girl with a Group Two consciousness. At school, I resided near

Group One-ers with the confidence of a tender slim weed in a well-tended Victory garden. The heavy hand of strict upbringing lifted me in my fear from the disgrace of being just average but dumped me stranded at the outer boundary of B marks without guidance for growth into the smart-kid crop. I was a sprout at the edge, rooted in abeyance, in dormancy.

On the other hand, the powerful elusive free spirit of Dance soared without restraint.

I stood near the window in the room that served as "parlor" that historical day in 1947 when I learned to jitterbug. I wound up my portable phonograph and put on a 78. My older sophisticated girlfriend demonstrated the step. (Much later I heard it labeled "swing." Too cool a name, too smooth. "Jitterbug" fit me, stifled energy finally finding its wiggling way out.)

We stood opposite each other and held one hand each. Seriously, step right, left follow, weight shift and shift again, over and over until it was perfected. I grin now remembering that it was the first time I felt dance power, that rush when music, the catalyzer, releases momentum that has marked time within us. Movement swept my soul to the boundary of my body, in turn the catalyst. I danced with abandon; I had no choice but to do so. Movement freed is infinity and it cannot stop. Our part is to enter the flow, shine in our rapture, and feel ourselves full.

Tendrils of Dance had beckoned me, the weed in the wings. Drawn forward I flourished. Side by side, roots intertwining, we converged as one, Dance and I. Unguided, nevertheless unstifled too in the years to come, this creature grew, developing thriving foliage and a strong center stem. "You've got good rhythm," my mother called once over her shoulder. Just as my long wild hair cut repeatedly grew back thicker, so did this complex being resist restraint. One day the question came that was repeated like a broken record through the years to follow: "Beverly, I

didn't know you could dance. *Have you been dancing all
your life?"*
   From that day on I never stopped jitterbugging, even
as the name changed to boogie woogie, to jig, to the twist,
to rock 'n roll. Together the dance and I became liberated.
Thank you teacher/friend whose face and name are gone
for that precious piece of the life-sized picture puzzle of
me.

* * *

REINCARNATION

Have you danced all your life?
Have you been dancing all your life?

    i came from out there, floating,
    immortality in dance,
    my ethereal cocoon;
    red womb but a formality

Have you danced all your life?
Have you been dancing all your life?

    i am time passing,
    the dance of life.
    not an "art"
    like a star pinned
    to the painted sky
    in afterthought.
    to dance *is* to live, Isadora,
    a star exploding centered in joy.
    ... movement is dance is life
    is time is movement is dance
    is life ...

Have you danced all your life?
Have you been dancing all your life?

> dispursed, a fading fireworks,
> expiring star dissolving through time.
> i'll dance invisible
> in the wind

* * *

THE BRICKER BROTHERS: A MINI MELODRAMA

or

ALAS, CONFIDENCE COMES LATE
(a true story)

TIME AND SETTING: Part I, 1980, Reminiscing about
High School Noon-time dances

Part II, 1949, The Freshman Hop

CHARACTERS: Narrator: Janice Bodel, Bosom confi-
dante to Beverly Sweetthing both in
1980 and in 1949.

Heroine: Beverly Sweetthing, who, having learned to jitterbug at the virtuous
age of 12, danced her ass off every
chance she got.

Heroes: The Bricker Brothers, Lenny in
Part I (alluded to) and Jack in Part II

Villain: Feeling of Female Powerlessness

PART I — REMINISCING 1980:

Narrator: (Curtain opens with Narrator downstage right. Stage is semi-lighted. Dim amber spot on Narrator Janice. She is a long-haired wife/mother who never embraced housewifery as a true 50's bride was supposed to have done. She wears jeans, huaraches, and an apron that reads, "I'd Rather be in Bed." She gyrates, nearly singing her speech rock-star style, around a microphone she holds.) "Lenny Bricker, wow! What a dude! Big man on campus — sexy, black curly hair, with that leather-like grease mystique." (Struts around in imitation of Lenny.) "He looked at people sideways, ya know? Man, to us fragile female freshmen this senior was not for *real*! Or maybe he was and we weren't. (Continues to swagger. Now addressing Heroine who is upstage center in semi-darkness.) "Anyway, it was at one of the noon dances, remember them? The clump of girls crouched in one corner, dig?" (Sassy-like, Janice acts out the scene.) "And Lenny comes right up to us, right straight to us, with that smile that turned on our juices, except we weren't having any of *that*, and he asked *you* to dance, to jitterbug. And you did — good, too." (She's excited.) "Man, were we all jea-lous!"

Heroine: (Bright white spot light comes up on Beverly who sits on a high stool upstage center in a pseudo lotus position. She's a writer/dance teacher recently from the roles of wife/mother who also never embraced housewifery as a true 50's bride was supposed to have done. In the interests of objectivity her costume makes an unbiased statement. She wears nothing and apparently has a shaven head. In both scenes she gushes.) "I don't believe it! Lenny Bricker asked little me? You're kidding! Why me?" (She blinks and fidgets nervously. The spot blinds her, carrying her back after many years to vulnerability and powerlessness.) "I don't know what to say. I wasn't like *that* — *fast!*"

Narrator: (Still gyrating.) "He probably knew you were a good dancer. But let's choose to believe he asked you because we always had '*it*' but didn't know it." (She whispers confidingly.) "For women in the 50's it was way under underground, baby!"

Heroine: "He asked me?" (Fluttering in tender modesty.) "I can't get over it. I was quiet and timid." (She gloats.) "The envy of everyone, huh; hmmmm." (Then getting in touch with her rage.) "Why the hell didn't I remember I'd been asked by the cream of the crop!" (Angrier.) "Hell, I sure remember all the negative stuff, god damn it." (Suddenly worried.) "I couldn't be a masochist, could I?" (Back of wrist to forehead she swoons as light fades to darkness and curtain closes slowly.)

PART II — FRESHMAN HOP 1949

Narrator: (Curtain opens with Narrator downstage right again, this time sitting on high stool, but facing upstage. She moves her upper body to the rhythm of Louis Prima singing "Yeah, Yeah, Yeah" in the background.) "Then came our first high school dance — far out! — hell, none of the rest of us even *went* — didn't get asked! Beverly did though." (She boogies off stage right as Beverly and Jack Bricker enter left. Like his older brother Lenny, Jack is also a status symbol. A lighter version of his brother — brown leather jacket, brown curly hair, sexy build. A charmer, a lady-killer (masculine Freudian expression) and quite a catch (likewise, feminine.) Beverly has long hair and wears a black straight skirt and a long-sleeved diaphanous blouse, a Pisces contradiction, pink for purity, see-through for sexy.)

Hero: "Want to dance?"

Heroine: "O.K." (Music louder, they jitterbug well together.)

Hero: (Another fast number) "Want to dance again?"

Heroine: "I guess so." (Slow music next. Billy Eckstine crooning "If They Made Me A King." Only in dancing does Beverly relax, and then not completely, unless it's a fast one.)

Hero: "You're a good dancer."

Heroine: "Tee Hee." (Smile, grin, help!)

Hero: "Hey, there's another fast one."

Heroine: "Yah!" (Louis Prima again playing and singing "She's My Good Boogdi Googi." A little more giggling and Beverly slips, with relief, into a hard boogie woogie. Fast curtain while they're dancing. Immediately Heroine appears through center curtain into a white spot light, clutching a white lace hanky and holding both hands to her bosom. Eyes upward, she scans the heavens, searching for the gods of power and self-confidence who, years later, finally emerge as goddesses from within her own breast, and she implores:) "But does he love me only for my dancing!"

(sad violin and slow, slow fade.)

oh brother!
oh Bricker Brothers!

* * *

Jefferson Dance Band's exchange show with Half
Moon Bay High. I was in the tenth grade and I do not for
the life of me know how I got into a four-girl "Blue Skies"
dance number. The date of this event occurred years and
years before I had reclaimed dance for myself. I was a girl
jock in P.E., not one of those I disdained as "dainties"
who took modern dance only to spare themselves the wet
hair of a swim meet. Also, generally I was shy, afraid,
cautious, good.

The entire "Blue Skies" episode is a mystery to me,
(did I volunteer, was I asked, who choreographed it, why
me?) the details of which are lost forever. All gone, except
the rush I received when I moved to that jazzy music. *That*
I will *never forget*: the excitement, my elation, the powerful delicious wisdom of my body, and, in retrospect, a
sense of the yet unconscious urgency to discover through
dance the quintessence of my being.

* * *

1950. The solid center of a century. A dark age of my
unguided evolution. I needed a candle. More light, even,
than the spark dance could provide. When I recall that
period of history I picture women of vague shapes and
muted activities in indistinguishable gray, and so far away
that I cannot hear them are the echoes of feet dancing. We
young women of that time, wrapped in shrouds, moved

mindlessly through the dim tunnel of our lives from students to wives to mothers, groping for more of something we could not name. With the passage of time some of us emerged to a brighter place of clear thinking, broader activities, creative personal work. And we returned, with renewed vigor and revised expectancy, to dance.

* * *

The year was '59; I was twenty-four. My dancing consisted of jitterbugging at the end of the counter that separated the living room from the kitchen, holding on tight with one hand as to a partner or for dear life. I never let go and passed into the next room. (Please hold my hand, Daddy.) I did not take dance classes. (In the '50s life after marriage was a bland, unending plateau.) Nor did I dance in the company of others. (Don't look at me; I'll become real.)

But I did yearn. The dancing on TV transfixed my insatiable eyes. In public, in silent agony, I did compare my latent abilities with those of every dancer on the floor. I did suppress regret.

Then, at counter's end one hot-jazz dancing day, the music "touched" me and I experienced a kind of satori, that mystical Eastern high place of enlightenment. From my center, through layers of body insulation, there ascended with force an energy so adrenalized that I shot through the top of my head in golden streaks that filled the room, passed through the ceiling and beyond, and returned enriched. I remember a frightening sense of power when I spoke to myself. "I can do anything!" I proclaimed aloud, flushed from dancing. I became normal again within seconds; nevertheless, I remained more aware, more anxious, more angry. I had changed forever. One never regresses completely.

I had received a sign: strong in dance, strong *period*! Often through the growing years to come the memory of this discovery would return sharply like the sudden, gorgeous dazzle of sun through a prism. And I wondered about other women's revelations. For me, definitive action was to follow much later.

* * *

I received a Wonder Woman book recently from a friend who calls me by that name. And, inspired by Amazon psychology and history, within ten days I smashed for myself the myth: Woman is Physically Weak.

Going way back, mothers of the sandbox set always called girls like me boys, with our bulging chests and straight backs. Always "A" marks in posture in junior high gym. Always the athletes who endured until dark. Disciplined upbringing fosters the stealthy nurturing of determination, steadfastness, strength. Strength. So our centers were strong. Women's centers *are* strong. But as good little girls, in early years we did not use our legs and arms to stray much or take much. We did not act out adventure. We did not stretch out and grab. As careless little mothers we both coddled and ignored our arms and legs. Improperly tended they atrophied.

Now I go to work to wreck a more specific myth: Woman is Limited by Weak Arms and Legs. I am dancing in earnest with the goal of strengthening. Already I can measure improvement. But even if I let down physically, the psychic gains are mine forever. For the deeper dimension of this strengthening endeavor is an exciting secret I barely whisper, scarcely have I discovered it. In the arms-and-legs myth how is one limited? Only in dance? Surely not. So when this myth, too, is smashed, how will we be unlimited? Take off like a rocket? No stopping us? Why not! As women of strength we may strive to realize

our hidden potential and act on spontaneous opportunity.
Giddy and giggling and totally pleased I tease myself
with a fantasy. Who knows, another Wonder Woman
maybe . . .?!

* * *

BODY EXPECTATIONS, AND LACK OF

Spine strong as steel,
a driven spike to the brain;
pain should she languor,
dare to let down.

Driving, drive drive.

Shoulders are holding.
Chest must support.
Vulnerable belly cuz
she thought it should be.
Hips and ass sassy though.

Holding, hold hold.

But arms thin as spindles;
the skin starts to sag.
Hands a weak squeeze
from seasons' not taking.
Legs heavy nothings
when feet want to fly;
lax from a lifetime
of taking her nowhere.

Taking, take take.
Taking!
Take!
Take!

* * *

It was Fall of 1964. Eighteen years I am still mad at what that damn man said. That damn damn black man who taught jazz in the morning to housewives like me coming out towards dance finally. He grinned all the time, slavering with condescension, until we laughed with him, too needy to know it was at ourselves.

And finally, the remark, through a sneer two wrinkles near hatred of our sex, our color, and mostly of our audacity to dance. "All right ladies, from the top again so when you're drunk on New Year's Eve you can really do your stuff!"

* * *

As a friend of mine says, "I can dance; you can dance." There are no required rites of passage to say *I am a dancer.*

Today I told an historian I was writing a book on dance. He inferred that inclusion of the philosophy of well-known dancers both past and present would be necessary for authenticity. I agreed, but felt increasingly uneasy with the idea. Days later in an angry flex, I stretched my body as in strong dance and cracked to a million pieces the steadily hardening mantle of authority before it smothered me again. "That is exactly what I will *not* do," I exploded, "invalidate my own dance wisdom!"

We women who love to dance, who create in dance, who actualize ourselves through dance, who communicate in dance, who reach our centers through dance, who express ourselves with dance, who meditate in dance — *we women are dance authority*. As in ancient cultures, dance is an integral part of our daily existence. Somewhere I read a book in which the author said her heroines were not women remote from her life but those other ordinary ones whom she had touched daily. If, like our sisters, we love dance and do dance, if we give any consistent part of our valuable energy to it in any form, whether or not we earn money from it, *we are dancers*.

In this book I am willing to share information gathered outside myself to support views I hold on dance. I am *not* willing to drop a famous name from any era so that its presence gives credence to my words. Attitude and philosophy regarding personal dance experience must emanate from within each of us. We unknown women dancers make our own dance histories. We are the authority we need to know and trust.

* * *

FRIDAY AFTERNOONS 1972

Isadora Duncan classes
trembling act of metamorphose.
Chrysalis of silk at throat,
taut, becomes a silken scarf
and slips to shoulders,
fringe like fingers
flung in reaching.
Oh filmy friend of iridescence
teach me how to flow
like your blur of colors
one on other
that seem a mirror
in slippery surrender
opening in space.

I stop then fast
tread air in panic
resist becoming a "duncan dancer."
Retie the scarf
suppress its splendor,
afraid again the butterfly
against the wind
won't flow with current
to unknown places,
fluttering wild
treading, treading time for now . . .

* * *

Audition. Literal definition: a hearing. A hearing, a judgement; authority, validation; acceptance, rejection. I was going to a dance audition. The child within one whose worth for so long has been subjected to sadistic scrutiny and condemnation by a looming, menacing authority figure often perpetuates, from habit, the ritual of judgement by others. Masochistically I offered myself to the block again. Angry fool grasping air instead of power.

The night before the dance audition I had a dream. I was in a contest where I needed to stand on a white pedestal facing the male judges. A slight breeze blowing gently through my skirt, blouse, and hair made me feel pretty, free, flowing. I thought, this is a cinch because I have much physical confidence. I felt fantastic and knew I would win. Then a woman judge asked if those were varicose veins in my legs. Yes. She disapproved. Shaken, I said veins had nothing to do with the quality of me. She said, you're not so young. I said that wasn't a criteria for entering the contest. She left me. I felt lonely. Later she saw me and said, I must tell you, you are the one most favored by the judges.

Apparently I had hoped someone at the dance audition the following day (a man, a woman, father, mother, sister, brother, husband, lover, anyone) would validate my dream, verify what I knew but kept forgetting, that I was special, at least o.k. The condition of low self-esteem in childhood carries with it a legacy. We such women inherit the compulsion to set goals towards which we strain to test our unworthy selves. Like my woman friend who after years of frenetic applying finally was accepted to medical school, only to decline. Ah, another plateau, a moment's rest.

Years ago as a very young adult I was using another kind of audition to take my parents' authoritative place. The bitter-sweet excitement of theater try-outs. I hated them. Like the good pain of massage on knotted muscles. I kept going back. Relentlessly my eyes haunted the director's inscrutable face for something that felt like love, a part in the play! (I retired from Community Theater work after I got the lead in a comedy. My timing was perfect in more ways than one.)

I went to the audition the next day, not to dance of course. After all, I knew by then I was going so I might measure my growth, be a judge, choose the final judge. I had danced through years of strengthening. I would validate the dream myself. Somewhere along the way I had stopped grabbing air.

That night I had another dream. A theater try-out with the same director of long ago who seldom cast me. Instead of feeling nervous and anxious I experienced myself as calm, quiet, and confident, for I knew how the dream would end. I smiled as I watched him adjust his eye glasses to read the names of the chosen ones. He called my name. Of course I knew already that I was one of the winners.

* * *

Yesterday I splintered myself as we women do in a panic to realize our full potential. Changing roles and clothes all day in haste I sprang from dance teacher to publisher to writer. Rushing towards work like a child afraid of being left behind I dashed through dance class preparations. I attached "How to Self Publish" to the crook of my arm as a woman forever lugs laundry or groceries or another's pain. And I urged words to come forth like dragging a tired toddler home.

Forget it all and dance, I flashed! But the centrifugal force in a whirlwind drives one back and back again though she strains irresistibly to touch center.

dancing
writing
poetry unpub-
lished writing
about dancing lessons
hurry to write to publish
to create dance faster twisted
a Maypole of tangled colored-paper
thoughts dizzy claw it all to shreds

I went to bed exhausted and persevered through a dream of obstacles. Frantic at dream's end — car impelled towards ocean's setting sun — sky orange, then sienna, *late*. "Oh," I said accelerating, "I must have missed it by now." But I awoke myself abruptly before the sky darkened, so there was no ending. Out of both fear of failure and desire to control my personal destiny, my conscious self had intervened in the dream, taking responsibility for my life, my work.

So this bright morning systematically I send out my poetry manuscript again. I plan thoroughly the week's dance lessons. The sun will not set for a long time. And I write about the source that restores, the tool that makes us whole — I write about dance.

* * *

This morning multi-fibered fingers of tension, slim as reeds, strong as steel, mean and tight as a witch's whine, grip my spine and neck and wrap around the muscles in my shoulders.

A Berkeley party last night in an old fire house converted to living space and sculptor's quarters, spacious with dark corners and intimate rooms. An un-Hollywood version of the hippie party from the movie, "Midnight Cowboy." Nobody knew anyone else but the band was good so we communed through dance. Dozens and dozens of people and still room to move — a dancer's fantasy fulfilled.

I never hurt the day after dancing, but maybe I was nervous in that atmosphere, tension being psychologically induced. Anyway, the thing that bothered me during the evening was a different physical problem. My left hip joint was aching. At times like that — when we women get tired before the dancing is done or we are out of breath or do not get that second burst that sends us moving through the night — we become jagged fragments of fear. "What if?!" we cry. What if I do not get enough dancing before my body stops? What if I am not fulfilled? What if I am not valued? Or loved? What if I am lonely? Or die? And the spinning of years' worth of self-confidence melts away like a little girl's cotton candy. *Well, what if?* I hold my breath in a moment of suspense, and exhale with relief. *Well, so what!* Luckily the panic passes more quickly each time it occurs. Perhaps some day it will not return at all.

So this morning I massage the skin of my left hip, pressing lovingly into my padded self. We must nurture our bodies, remembering to appreciate the vital part they play in the spirituality of dance. And we must know that only fear can reduce us.

Who knows, like my neck and shoulders, maybe this hip, too, is a psychological hurt.

* * *

Mirisol played the music, Brazilian, bubbling boiling hot. Maracas rattling tremble rumble bubble bubble rumbling drums rolling voices hot humid waves of rhythm. Chicachicachicachica brrrrrr rah!

She danced alone; the people ogled. She shook and dipped and threw her head. Others of us feared to join her though it was a public club. So at the tables feet or hands or heads danced in little jabs from bodies gone rigid with imprisoned rhythms. Anxious dancers wasting energy repressing energy. And stiffled movement continued to strain towards maniacal abandon.

I could not stand it any longer. I surrendered myself to my own shaking shoulders, undulating hips, arms that flowed, hula hands with accent beat. Occasionally, I withdrew from this meditative dance to glance at the other person with whom I shared the floor. It appeared she was a well-trained dancer for her body was flexible while her movements were tightly controlled. She wore street clothes, pants and full-sleeved blouse with wide cuffs that gave her dance a look of freedom. She performed not for herself. I felt like part of an audience even as I danced. Though I respected her privacy, I hoped she would respond to my presence so we might exchange moments of movement. But she never looked back at me or into the band or the people sitting. She was hidden behind a one-way mirror that afforded her protection, but she could not see out.

We continued dancing, each alone, never crossing the line to the other's half of the floor. Shaking, rattling, reaching, twirling — ending hot and happy, exhausted, excited. Still hoping to share, I went to her, touched an arm, made a remark. She said thank you as if she were accepting a long-stemmed red rose.

When I sat down with my friends, one of them did a critique on her and me, and I knew he was voicing what others were thinking. I realized people watch to judge, not to enjoy. I did not care. I knew she would be judged the "better" dancer. I did not care about that either. *That all felt good!* I had loved the music. I had moved with my need. Rejected by the other, I had valued my own dance more. In the end, I felt positive, outgoing, loving, confident. Once again, as my guide for measured growth, Dance had stepped with me to another stage of self-actualization.

Smiling to myself, I withdrew the rose, snapped short its stem, and slipped it in my hair!

* * *

I nearly always dance barefooted. But last week at the local pub, delirious with Friday Night Fever, I danced in high-heeled boots. They tipped me off balance; I leaned back to re-center. And when I did this my personality changed. With my weight back my pelvic thrust itself up and under, turning the inner thighs out. My knees bent slightly. I felt ready to spring though the jungle, or be sprung upon. I was centered in my crotch.

A crotch-centered personality is not sensual like dance is. Black leather square-heeled lace-up boots may be erotic or pornographic or militarily s-and-m-ish, but sensual like a Grecian garment of silk chiffon they are not. In ordinary walking wear these boots protect me from the world, vulnerability swathed in leather. I can bind them tight as Chinese slippers, my social growth contained. In dancing I am protected a step further. Feet corsetted to the knees means preservation in separation. I dance alone though bodies surround me. To a beat that beats like distant drums. A disco beat, a clunk, clunk, clunk. A tied up tight, an uptight tied, protect oneself with hard, glazed eyes. One gains security in submitting to the tyranny of the beat. Not to be confused with Pulse.

Pulse is an undulating flow which, like the belly of an Arabic dancer, invites one to be free. This leads to responsibility of touch with others. One rips her laces then, like stripping gears; kicks off the boots as chains and shields are shed. And dances — barefooted.

* * *

bare feet dancing

sinewy strong
bare feet working
cling determined
then swift release
and sensing gently
descend again

* * *

At some time every woman nurtures her secret version of the fantasy I held dear for years. Our social need creates a warm place in the mind that is cushioned with caring others in a flexible network of secure community. We continue to conjure up the idea of this cozy retreat whenever our befriending of ourselves is insufficient.

In *my* lonely years I dreamed of having a salon — a central gathering place in which, as historically defined, interesting people of all sorts would come together casually but regularly to share of themselves. The assorted versions of this fantasy hold for us the concept that we are securely in the center of society and not at the fringe, that we are in the powerful central flow of human interaction and not at the stagnant shallow edge. What we do not see is that Dance is at the shallow edge with us.

In lonely times Dance is there always though we may not know its use. Press a baby close and twirl, frolic gaily with our children; dance in streets, at clubs and schools, folk and square and dozens more called "social dancing." No accident this, that the first dance of the evening is called a "mixer" to sanction the need to interact. How sad when we count the times we declined fearfully, yet continued to grope for the net or line of interconnection. As passing years bequeath to us a small degree of wisdom for perceiving that which may enrich our lives, Dance becomes luminous.

Whimsically, I had persisted in remaining open to my Salon fantasy, breathing it forth in times of need, visualizing its elusive form, and letting it escape again. Then one day when Dance was shining brightest for me I realized my dream. *I drew together people to dance — my Sunday Salons.* For two years of an evening twice a month on Sundays at seven there came a select few who loved to dance, a changing group with a nucleus of dance devotees. A warm den of social sharing: food, drink, and talk; dance, dance, and dance! In helping fulfill this fantasy, once again Dance had reminded me there is no limit to the ways we may provide successfully for ourselves if we but trust in our power to do so.

* * *

When we are ready to see a truth about ourselves we find it fits as snugly as a leotard and feels just as secure and familiar. We had marked time until we were ready to slip into it. Home one night recently from social dancing at the Last Day Saloon I took responsibility for some personal dance truths. First, *I prefer myself to others as a dancing partner.* Dancing is a private form of self-expression for me, as it is for many other women. Greedily, I begrudge giving away to another any part of the dance. I make this statement clean, wiping away smudgy thoughtprints of guilt about relating and communicating.

So many people with whom one dances are sorely limited in their ability to move improvisationally. Why should any of us share static energy in someone else's space, when, alone, we can reinvest our resources into ourselves to create a greater degree of expression. If a woman is independent in other aspects of life, why must she be forced in a dance situation to form a symbiotic connection with another. One should dance with others only if one *chooses* to become involved in the transcending flow of improvisation, where neither "should" nor "need" are prerequisites for the dance creation.

Next, I acknowledged two seemingly contradictory attitudes I hold. *I love to dance for friends.* Their admiring, attentive eyes perceiving the greatest subtleties of my movement and mood inspire and nurture me. I meet a gaze wholeheartedly, smiling, happy in the supreme pleasure of sharing what I am with those I love. Contrariwise, at the local pub *I recoil at the probing eyes of strangers.* (Even as I tell my students noone really cares how we dance.) In a public dance we reveal so much of who we are through the parts of our bodies that it is painful for me to give away any more of myself than I do, so I often avoid exchanged glances. It seems we may be as timid with strangers as we are bold with friends. I am. I cannot prevent people from taking with their stares my hips, my hands, my head, or my breasts. But I will not feel ashamed of not wanting to look at *them*, especially if eyes are the mirror of the soul. They *cannot* have that, too.

* * *

When I have danced the night before in the morning I am warmer, lighter, thinner, rosier. I am prettier. I smile more. In walking the air supports me. In talking I gesture fluidly. I never nourish beyond my needs. The sun is wonderful; the wind is wonderful; they can't touch my skin enough. I write with absorption; I exist in euphoria. I am a stream of consciousness, a living example of the first Law of Motion, filling the spaces along the way to overflowingly bountiful capacity.

* * *

My highest state in dance occurs when I *am* the music. The first time this amazing phenomenon happened I was dancing alone at home to blues. Relaxed, I was able to listen with an intensity which absorbed me into the sounds. Outside pressures and considerations of other time and space fell away. I danced wholly centered, mind and body, within the music.

Then the second step towards becoming the music took place. I lost awareness of my body as a separate entity responding to the music in terms of feet, hands, or hips moving with little vacuums of time in between the hearing and the moving to assimilate the dance with the music. Instead, there was a simultaneous happening: the presence of the music and my reaction to it in body movement existed at once, together. I believed that not the slightest fissure of time or space intersected this existential stream. And yet, even at that point of development I had a deep knowledge that my body was still in control of the movement, not an intellectual knowledge (I did not think about it) rather, an intuitive awareness. Though I felt extremely centered, the three entities — music, movement, body — yet remained separate, with the body in charge. So, on second look there *were* imperceptible fissures after all.

Then something amazing happened. I went a step further and the experience solidified. Suddenly, my mind's eye saw the shapes and lines created by the presence of the music. Certainly they were not physical shapes. They did not rest upon the floor or set upon the couch. Nevertheless, they were real. And I *was* those shapes, in that my body as it danced took their form. I was the thin, undulating song of a harmonica, the rosy, round circle of a drumbeat.

At this point my mind did not direct my body to move. The three entities of music, person, and movement were, indeed, joined at last, each taking equal responsibility for the action. Instantly the music sounds became shapes and my mind watched with delight like an interested spectator as my body re-created the shapes. *I had become the music.* My essence consisted of the flow of sound, movement, body. I had transcended my normal consciousness state. Without directing, I observed my body dancing automatically, for it had become the music by assuming the sound shapes.

Explaining this phenomenon is like trying to describe how one hears "purple." Evidently I am not the only dancer to have merged with the music to become one entity. In Myron and Constance Nadel's *"The Dance Experience,"* Alexander Sakharoff is quoted from his *Relexions sur la Musique et sur la Danse.* He says, "We — Clotilde Sakharoff and I — do not dance *to* music, or with musical accompaniment, we dance *the music.*" The person who taught him to dance this way he says was Isadora Duncan, whose dance philosophy I much admire. According to Sakharoff, for Isadora there was no "dance music" but only pure music rendered as dance. I see this as another way of describing my experience of transcendence to the state of fused music, body, and movement.

Alexander Sakharoff further says that music and dance are as closely related as poetry and prose, that is, two major forms of one art. And though existence of this intimate relation has been repudiated by some dancers, nevertheless, this idea supports the authenticity of my own experience in this matter.

A scientist, Barbara Brown, has written a book, *New Mind, New Body*, which is about bio-feedback. In one section she discusses the futuristic possibilities of translating brain wave activity to music and art. "Some laboratories, including my own," she says, "have already developed primitive forms of bio-music. The concept of transforming biological signals into aesthetically acceptable music or art forms theoretically appears to offer exciting new forms of therapy and therapeutic approaches." She elaborates upon the idea. "Music and/or art produced by the functions of the mind and body and faithfully translated do not merely represent the person's being, they literally *are* the person's being."

My interest in this statement is that it relates to my dance transcendence experience, verifying my discovery of the changeability of my essence from a mind/body state to a music state. I did not create the music originally as Barbara Brown discusses. I changed already existing sound (the music) to mind states that my body translated to moving shapes. I reversed the process or supplemented the cycle. But regardless of the direction of the flow's electrical energy I am convinced some of us dancers can and do become the music.

* * *

MEDITATION

Golden light,
velvety soft satin
candle-flicker light.
Golden light bulbs, pear shaped.
Pillow-shaped cushioned
cotton liquid light.
Liquid flames, fire changing
luminating my oiled body
fluid with the music
in undulating dance
arms breasts belly hips
shine in firelight alive.
Singing sounds around me
waves so thick I finger them,
so delicate they dissolve into skin
and I am the music; I *am* the light.

My essence slipping from me
fills the room like golden vapor
towards, absorbed by
a thousand watching eyes.
Then flowing joyous, a genie-mist,
back through dancing fingertips
to golden center light of
my fine translucent being.

* * *

It was a down day despite the sun. A disjointed, odd-angled, chopping-board day, intensified by the street fair's flamboyance. Short, sharp activities assaulted me. Garish colors jetted from the street; I squinted for protection. I alternated between semi- and unconscious mental states, walking through mini moods first of numbness, then of vulnerability bright as pain. I wandered heavily to the crowd's pace, clearing my throat a few times, hoping instead to clear my mind of its groggy, sunshiny confusion where nothing matched, fitted, or fused.

After a block I got snagged in a group at a feather stall. I touched some feathers. Liquidy-light, delicate and soft, they soothed me. I breathed in deeply and out fluttered the feathers in my head, settling before me to tickle my fingertips and massage the palms I slid across all the muted colors.

I breathed again, my vision cleared; I picked a feather barrette and clipped it in my hair. Brown, tan, and gold. The hue of the feathers matching the color of my hair was the link, like a lock and key. Brown, tan, golden on the ends, the beginning of a flowing connection, a dance back to life. Lightly I tossed my hair; the air supported it.

Clear now, I opened like wings, attracting the sun and allowing its unblocked energy to run fluid through feathers and hair, charging me completely before it passed into swirls like tentacles that encircled my space and drew me to connect with the perfectly fused pattern of movement all around.

* * *

"When we are completely immersed in what we are doing and lose a sense of self and time we are in the state of *flow*." This definition is that of psychologist Mihaly

Csikszentmihalyi (hereafter, Dr. C) from a June, 1976 article in *Psychology Today*. "A person gains a heightened awareness of his physical involvement with the activity, and his enjoyment is enormously enhanced." A rock dancer told Dr. C: "If I have enough space, I feel I radiate energy into the atmosphere. I become one with the atmosphere."

Dr. C. interviewed one hundred twenty-five people in a variety of activities and found the greatest reward was the altered state of being that occurred when they were most enjoying the activity — that altered state of *flow*. One rock climber put it this way: "You are so involved in what you are doing you aren't thinking of yourself as separate from the immediate act."

> Five dancers like gently tangled seaweed
> at ocean's edge, ebbing, rising together to
> slow continuous music. Bodies warm, and
> breath; backs brush, an arm 'round waist,
> then gone to join another's hand. Coercion
> surrendered to an existential ocean and
> beyond the dancers' boundary space all else
> fades away.

This is successful improvisational dance. We allow ourselves to enter flow in movement, taking dance from the cerebral realm to a physical place of total absorption. It is transcendence through a stream of energy to confidence and communion.

In their book, *Modern Dance*, Gay Cheney and Janet Strader discuss improvisational movement. It is interesting that their guides to doing successful improvisational dance resemble closely Dr. C's discoveries regarding flow. For instance, Dr. C. found that people in flow undergo an extreme focusing of attention on the activity, the concentration becoming progressively intense and automatic. "The game is a struggle, but the concentration is like breathing — you never think of it," said an expert chess player. "Your body is awake all over," a dancer explained. Likewise, regarding improvisational movement Cheney and Strader say dancers become totally "in" the dance. "In" is a state in which all outside considerations, including time, are less important than the improvisation. You are not concerned with how you look, what is coming next, or if your toe is pointed. As with the chess player's concentration, "you never think of it."

In flow there is no sense of self, according to Dr. C. A tennis player in flow is not bothered by such thoughts as "am I doing well?" If the moment is split so that the player perceives his action from the outside, then flow halts. Similarly if a dancer slips out of "in" she loses her flow. To achieve and retain the state of being "in," that is, to surrender one's sense of self to the flow, Cheney and Strader suggest focusing elsewhere — on the movement, the quality of movement, the timing. I suggest my students focus on tangible items, like another dancer. Or on their hands, in a hand-improvisation dance. Physical props work too; scarves are super.

Another factor in flow, according to Dr. C, is the clarity of response that the individual gets from the activity, the internal sense of rightness. A basketball player interviewed said if he has a great game he doesn't realize it until it is all over. He flows with his expertise action without stopping to analyze how he is doing. Likewise, dancers in a successful improvisational piece are so connected to the movement and to each other, so totally "in," that not until the dance ends do they snap out of their revery, smile at each other and exclaim, "hey, that was extra special!" Cheney and Strader say that until your body and mind function as one at the same instant, you remain mentally on the outskirts of the dance. You are not "in" the dance; you experience no sense of rightness or centeredness. You are simply watching, not flowing.

Finally, Dr. C. says there is a sense of control when one flows. Said his chess player, "although I am not aware of specific things, I have a general feeling of well-being and that I am in complete control of my world." Flowing in dance creates for one a fantastic sense of self-confidence, a self-control, a powerful connection with the flow of life. Cheney and Strader put it this way: "One of the important results of dance improvisation is the development of your sensitivity — sensitivity to time, to space, to energy, to other people, to motion." Most of all, one develops a sensitivity to oneself.

> Five dancers swirl, hearing the music's nuances
> not with their ears but kinesthetically.
> Responding, flowing, they surrender their
> bodies 'til body and music as two separate
> parts fuse to become a third entity — dance.
> Time slips by; background blurs from excited
> to quiet dance, from solid to liquid response.
> Moving in and out of space and rhythm, no one
> leading, no one following, they touch, they
> part, return and blend.

The famous writer, Anais Nin, was also a dancer. In Volume 1 of her diary she, too, talks about flow. "I used to build cathedrals, cathedrals of sentiment, for love, for love of men, for love as prayer, love as communion, with a great sense of continuity and detail and enduringness. *Build against the flux and mobility of life, in defiance of it.*[1] Then with Henry,[2] with June,[3] with analysis with Rank, I began to flow, not to build. Yesterday, flow

1.   my italics
2.   Henry Miller
3.   June, his wife

seemed so easy. . . . letting life flow one may attain states of nirvana, dreaminess, beatitudes of another kind."

The day I bought the feather barrette was one in which I experienced my cathedrals melting and carrying me into the flux of life, just as dance does. "How well it blends with the color of your hair," a woman had said. And I thought of paintings by Renoir and Klimt where life blends and flows. I had focused on my brown barrette and slipped totally "in" my improvisational dance of passing through the street, of flowing with the crowd.

* * *

I am partner to powerful Wind dancing through ice-bright blue sunny Sunday at the bandstand. She flurries in and out row upon row of green benches. I am grateful for the sun. Selection No. 1, *El Matador*, a march by Carazo, brisk, fitting her mood. The entire company joins Wind in her dance: colorful scarves, silvery hair, branches of trees, dry, fallen leaves. Only the birds resist, by so doing creating contrasting choreography.

Now, by Berloiz, *Roman Carnival Overture*, matching the atmosphere. People crisscrossing create a kaleidoscope like a vivid embroidery, a liquid tapestry, patterning, re-patterning.

Soon, *Symphony Nine* by Dvorak, stronger sounds accompany Wind's sharper turns. The design blurs with her capriciousness. I close my eyes and see her rush raw past my cheek. The drums beat hard, the sun beats hard upon my face. Slowly, through half-closed lids I again catch color.

Music ending, Wind is exiting. The dance is over but for the finale. To last chords a great group of waddling pigeons flutter suddenly straight up into the sky. Wind is high; I catch my cue and move on with the tempo of the shifting flux.

* * *

An exercise in creative writing is that one read a particular author directly before proceeding with one's own work and, invariably, the author's style will influence the writing. Likewise, I have been watching much ballet lately and, ironically, I am off balance physically in my own dancing as a result. In dancing I center mid-body, as do many other people. For us, movement arises from an ever-bountiful energy source, mysterious and ageless, tapped to the force of the perfect universe. Dancing, to us, is not just an art; it is nature's rhythm. When we move in unison with life's pulse our dance is effortless, as if we are rocked by the hand of Mother Nature. We are centered.

Though, like others, I pay homage to the superb gymnastic strength of a ballet dancer, I continue to ask, "in what part of her body is she centered? In her toes? Her head?" Her body is a flawless precision machine, as soothing to the eye to watch as is the dependable reoccurance of pistons exact, forward and back. But for all its technical perfection a machine cannot be centered.

Where in her body is the bottomless pot of golden energy into which the ballet dancer may dip and come out well-balanced and renewed? I sense she has, instead, a supply of hoarded energy distributed throughout her body in exact even proportions, locked tight at the precise boundary, her skin, and burned up only in measured meters to propel the fine machine. No energy amount is lavished in spilled-over, electrified swirls to interconnect with other life-giving currents.

In my dance, I wish to release, not keep. For energy begets energy. Like others, I strive for fluidity, a stream that ties dance, one of life's entities, to the next encounter like beads on a silken string. We such dancers will not cut carefully shaped pieces out of space or out of life, but rather, we pour and flow, allowing soul to pass through infinity and return in cyclic repetition to our centers from which we may continue to give forth.

* * *

Soul versus technique. What a pity most dancers do not have both.

A dancer drills; she labors long, sweats, gets skill and fame. Ho hum . . .

Another dancer simply extends an arm and we are dazzled by its aura.

Isadora Duncan had soul. Of the Alvin Alley Company, Judith Jamison, evoking tearful emotional response, has it too.

In the February 3, 1978, issue of the San Francisco Chronicle, Klarna Pinska, maid for many years to Ruth St. Denis, famous pioneer of modern dance, says in essence: Style and creativity were the most important considerations for the dancers then. If only we had dancers now with the style of the old times and the bodies of today's women . . .

Ah, yes!

Merce Cunningham, a leading American modern dancer, gives us a sampler to embroider, hang high, and live by:

Too much creativity makes for a flabby body.
Too much technique, for a robot.

* * *

Early Spring, time of birth and renewal, 1975.

I named the first workshop "Let's Boogie!" It was conceived accidentally when I was forty.

To regress, when first I discovered and temporarily discarded Isadora Duncan in 1972, via the San Francisco Neighborhood Arts Program of free Duncan technique classes, I had not reclaimed dance yet for my life. Neither had the other closet dancers I knew. Our busy lives were alike in that we had held dance as a last priority and finally, through lack of self-expectation, we let go. In retrospect, we should forgive ourselves. I do. I was working nights full time and going to college days, plus maintaining house, husband, and daughters. But I was drawn to the Duncan idea of freedom in movement.

So I had not let go entirely. Three years later in 1975. (after getting a B.S. degree in Early Childhood Education finally and teaching nursery school) I was teaching my own dance classes based on freedom in movement and improvisation. The impetus to dance again, fostered by those past Friday afternoon Duncan classes, had emerged through rhythms gone dormant; and it gained strength with momentum. First I danced alone daily at home to classical and jazz-rock.

oh god i'm doin' it, i'm dancin'!

It was time to come out for good. I went to the Women's Center in San Mateo with a little voice. "I'd like to bring women together to dance."

"Certainly. How much will you charge?" Money! for dancing!

At that point the anxiety of confinement ended. "Let's Boogie!" was born and grew robustly into a new career.

* * *

"You sure love teaching don't you," Sue smiles as I cut through the kitchen like a shining, sharp knife plunging the center of their warm cozy dinner.

"The class went great. Of course I love it!" I say, dropping my record case and coat. From my aura of dance energy charged reactions flash like sparks: flip of the hair, flick of a hand, snap crackle pop, d'ya wanna dance cha cha cha!

The others sit snug, nodding, what a nice kooky lady.

How many people get paid for doing that which they love. I keep reminding myself I am working. And I do work. Dancing harder than any student does, I flex, flow, and twist, my teaching technique in improvisational movement being such that I furnish a model so the dancers will give themselves permission to move outrageously. A school of shining purple fish, we glide and slide, scales like sequins, an energy exchange, slick, quick through medium of space and time. So, like a fish in and out of water, I alternate between surrendering to the flow of movement and withdrawing to observe, guide, comment, encourage, and reassure the students they are becoming more powerful and free with each session.

Later I will be spent. Later I will lie heavy on the pillows by the fire, limbs lazy, the energy finally having retreated to my core, its resting place. I will leave the dinner mess until morning and put out the cats (dammit where're you hiding Boots?). I will drag myself to bed early, again missing the re-run of Saturday Night Live, oh well. Sighing, I will wonder, as other dancers do, how long I can keep this up, and in two minutes I will be dead asleep.

* * *

Attendance at my summertime workshops has a whimsical on-again off-again quality. In summer people permit their own capriciousness, flowing hedonistically with moods and weather. So it was not surprising to me that Eleanor was the only woman to come to the last night of the July Improvisational Rock Workshop. In true improvisational spirit I decided to alter the planned lesson and give her whatever help she wanted with her dancing.

Eleanor is an open, smiling, physically fit woman of sixty years, who reacts twinklingly to new ideas. For awhile we worked on some foot things and other general stuff she suggested. The theme for the last session was to have been "self-confidence." So near the end of the hour I sat down and directed her to dance while I watched. She moaned only slightly through her smile; I knew she could handle it.

I pointed out the important difference between dancing "while I watched" and dancing "for me." I explained that dancing in front of someone else is easy when one is dancing expressly for oneself. In rock dancing one must please herself, not another. I reassured her that the more one dances before others, the more comfortable one becomes. I told her to remember the improvisational tools stressed in past classes: getting in touch with the music through concentrated listening, feeling centered in whatever part of her body the music "settles into," and giving herself permission to move with that centered feeling. I played a cut of innovative rock-jazz from "The Snow Goose" by a group named *Camel*.

What a teacher's joy it was watching Eleanor! She closed her eyes and let the music come to her instead of rushing out and past it. She listened and swayed gently. By degrees she moved until her feet were taking her around the room. She centered in her legs and bent them much, letting her arms follow along in their own way. Her head danced, and she leaned side to side from the waist. She did a gentle dance in which she was totally absorbed. She forced nothing. Spontaneously, she and the music together had created a third entity — her dance.

She finished flushed and radiant, yet calm and sure as a person of power. One sensed her self-satisfaction. She had made the workshop complete for us both. In watching Eleanor dance I had witnessed someone making a connection with herself, her world, another person, and her deep creative powers. She had released vital energy through her dance, which, by way of infinite recycling, recharged herself and me.

* * *

IMPROVISATION

Keith Jarrett I was asleep
in morning sun when notes
like leafy messages
from *Koln's* side one
came fluttering through the window
in perfect purity —
inspiration for honesty
in my dance.

My body's gestures:
    movement repeated
    'til it finds new self.
Your creative absorption:
    a chord over and over
    'til it flows into another.

Earthy in your intensity,
in my anxiety to dance the truth.
Spiritual the sounds your hands make,
the lines made by mine.

Communion invited, I read in that message;
I danced through your essence.
And though we've not met
I know you Keith Jarrett.

* * *

The Creative Dance for Women Workshop is new, so the lessons, like women growing, are in the process of evolving. The characteristics of developmental stages are the same in all new encounters. In the Improvisational Rock Workshops I went through the process of testing an idea, altering and enhancing it, succeeding or failing, until I had the system that worked best. The process is understandable. Nevertheless, for two weeks only one person has attended Creative Dance class. I ask myself what is wrong, especially recalling the women's breathless enthusiasm at hour's end. Why are they afraid to return? What do we risk in trying something new?

Half of the ten students have used the class productively as a vehicle for giving themselves permission to experiment, to free their bodies, to evolve. In a world of painting by numbers it is difficult for us women to initiate action without a guide or guru to say what to do. Some of us need so much more structure than others. *We all want to dance.* But in some cases childhood spontaneity of movement has been so cripplingly abused by tradition, convention, propriety, and fear that I wonder if we will ever risk the rescue of this self-renewing trait.

In teaching dance I find that women who live in particular locales (cities) are less inhibited generally than those who reside in other places (suburbs.) I was delighted to experience the exception in this week's Creative Dance class. Fran is a young suburban grandmother of trim fi-

gure and neatly teased and sprayed hair. She is the one woman who came to class. She displayed sympathy for me.
Sorrow showed in her big brown cocker spaniel eyes when
she said, "those women don't give themselves a chance.
They're afraid to try." Right on, sister! "I think they want
you to show them certain steps. Sometimes it is hard for
me too; then I just go off on my own and try to enjoy the
music and do what I can."

My head bobbed in agreement. I could have kissed her.
What a personally powerful woman she is. And I thank her
for putting me in mind again of my own special talent,
that of reuniting women with dance.

So next week I will "renumber" the lesson. All of us
deserve to be met at the place "we're at." It feels o.k. The
growth process. Evolution. We are all midway through the
process. So is my Creative Dance course. It feels o.k.

* * *

Ego: I keep teaching in safe places, like a professor in an
ivy dancehall.

Id: But a teacher is useless unless she is a dancing step
ahead of her students.

Ego: Ah, but such challenge in the unknown — the discovery, connection, communion, excitement!

Id: . . . the anxiety, the research, the planning, the
failure.

Ego: I will go there!

Id: . . . when I've time.

* * *

Correlations, correlations . . .

As in a steam bath, getting poison out of my pores. Went to a teachers' dance workshop and painfully sweated out some of *the poisonous juices of fear of*:

1. not executing choreography successfully
2. not being the most graceful
3. not being the most technically proficient
4. not being the most endurable

And, analogously, for I see these fears are symptoms indicative of broader anxieties in the lives of us women, *the poisonous juices of fear of*:

1. (not executing choreography successfully) *not being able to succeed creatively.*
2. (not being the most graceful) *not being physically attractive and healthy.*
3. (not being the most technically proficient) *not being a woman of personal worth.*
4. (not being the most endurable) *not being able to let go.*

Ah, another sharp dance step from heavy, foggy discontent to air of clear enlightenment.

* * *

A metaphor, a dream: the theme, the perpetual struggle for life's meaning. A journey from the familiar and secure into a labyrinth, where turn upon turn is like a reflection in a room of mirrors, the most distant image being the most depthful. In the dream the first rooms I entered were ordinary and led from one to another in a progressive predictable pattern, my having visited those realities many times. But the places were not satisfying. I was restless and anxious in them, like a woman caged. I passed through quickly, knowing my journey should not end in any of them. I escaped to outdoors (ah!), going up a hill (of course).

At this point in the dream my awareness changed from my being in a "mindstate" through the first rooms to a "bodymind state." My body assumed equal responsibility with my mind for behavior by forbidding the latter alone to plan future movements. This action resulted in a state of delightful improvisation, the kind I teach in my dance, where we respond at once with our whole selves to the stimulus presented to us.

In the dream this improvisational condition manifested itself in my doing an elfin-like dance through the natural setting of dirt path and greenery. At each turn, because the terrain changed, a spontaneous inspiration for new steps and movements took place. Around a shrub, a sunny circle to twirl in. Beside a low branch, my cool, quiet arms in a slower dance. Ahead, I leaped from rock to stone.

As a bodymind I lived in an existential moment. There was no thought of the path behind or the turn ahead. Rather, I felt great joy at moving in communion with all things immediately around me, be they called life or God or infinity.

Never mind that I reached a third consciousness, a spiritual one in which my essence arose and flew like a great misty cloud, demanding body to follow soul. Never mind, too, that I soared downhill and across water to my original starting point, perhaps to begin a new incarnation.

What *is* most pertinent about this dream is the implication that there is an analogy between women learning to improvise in dance and women learning to improvise with self-actualizing behavior in other parts of their lives. Though I kept sight of a future goal (I was moving toward the top of the hill) I responded eagerly through dance, with creativity and confidence, to the immediate day's

gift from life, the delightful surprise packages of unantici-
pated stimuli. Indeed, one's body and mind may join together to perform with exhilaration each moment's worth
of living in a most powerful stream of life consciousness.

* * *

Verily, I say to you, each teacher must deal with the
pressure from society and the demand of her own voice
that she should be "doing" instead of "teaching." Glowing
like a Biblical threat in the new world, a computerized
message wraps around and around her brain, *"Those who
can, do; Those who cannot, teach."* Bright as a demon
beacon sometimes, mercifully dimmed at other times, it
never fades altogether from her consciousness nevertheless.

But I say unto you, when we are ready for truth, wisdom, or beauty (and all three may be the same), it will be
there for us, whether it be a line from a poem, a remark by
a friend, or a lonely wildflower in the field. Likewise, in
the flash of a personal epiphany each woman will settle
the "teach-or-do" problem for herself when it is time to
do so. For me, seeing the written word, *"doing,"* gave me
clarity in understanding my position in this dilemna.

Firstly, we must recognize that in dance the traditional
interpretation of the word "doing" is analogous with that
of "performing." Yet, performing for others is not the
source of one's creative and spiritual satisfaction. Only the
essence of performance truly rewards us, that is, the act of
dancing, the "doing." This "doing" must exist for the private edification of the dancer, not for public approval. It is
often spontaneous, not planned. And, ironically, what is
more, the pleasure of "doing" may occur *during* the act of
teaching. So, let us not be frustrated by the sloppy blending of terms that confuse and deceive regarding true dance

needs.

Let me emphasize the dancing in my life and continue to practice the "doing" of it, as I have for years in many ways for the enrichment of my soul. Let every teacher think on how she may dance for herself by whatever means she may find to do so. Let us give the "doing" and the "teaching" equal importance in our lives, for each benefits us in its way; and we will continue to be in a state of grace. As we nurture others by giving through teaching, so be it that we may nurture ourselves by allowing dancing through its myriad ways of "doing" to come completely into our bodies and souls. Amen.

* * *

PART II

THE WORKSHOPS:
IMPROVISATIONAL ROCK DANCE
CREATIVE DANCE
DANCE YOGA-CIZE

Part Two

IMPROVISATIONAL
ROCK DANCE
WORKSHOPS

This section of *Power To The Dancers!*, like the preceding part, is valuable for both teachers *and* private individuals. It is for the woman who desires to obtain personal freedom and strength through dancing. And it is for that woman who believes she will develop the ability to be spontaneous and to improvise in her life by releasing the restrained dancer within her. Of course teachers will use the following workshops, but I ask the reader to remember that these classes emerged from my efforts to explore dance personally with other women *before I became a teacher*. Simply, I developed the original workshop from dance ideas I wanted to share *in dancing* with others. So, whether one is a woman alone helping herself to dance better or an instructor helping others, the workshops will be of interest to all.

Currently, I teach three adult dance workshops: Improvisational Rock, Creative Dance for Women, and Dance Yoga-Cize. But when I started teaching in 1975 at the Women's Center in San Mateo, California, I taught only Improvisational Rock Dance. I called the first workshop "Let's Boogie!" The leaflet description of the course read as follows:

> **Let's Boogie!** A six-week workshop in improvisational
> rock dancing. People often tell me they love to dance
> but either can't, or are embarrassed, or have no one to
> dance with. I was once such a woman. I would like to
> help others recapture the confidence and rhythm of
> childhood. There will be structured and unstructured
> activities for helping us loosen up and let go! We'll
> move to all types of music and we won't always be
> beautiful. Wear the "costume" you like to dance in.

Since 1975 the Improvisational Rock Dance Workshops
have evolved through many changes, but the purpose of
them has remained constant: *to give people the tools with
which they may permit themselves to improvise freely in
dance movement and to teach "release" rather than "control" of the body in dancing.*

In the beginning there were mini themes within the
framework of a six-week workshop. Each theme opened a
new variety of movement to the students. For example,
one week was devoted to Isadora Duncan; another, to African music. Of course a part of every session involved rock
and jazz music because the goal of the students was and
still is to develop enough expertise (I call it confidence)
to go out dancing, in short, to boogie.

Regarding the most important element of the courses,
building confidence, I would tell the women that if they
could don a toga as we did in class and glide Isadora Duncan fashion to Gluck's dances or improvise movement in
and around a straight-backed chair to music by Bach, they
could most certainly do a little innovative foot stompin'
and hip shakin' to a local rock group. In other words, the
class exercises were far more demanding in terms of personal dance improvisation than public social dancing ever
would be.

The first three classes of the Workshops emphasize dancing alone. In the second three emphasis is placed on beginning awareness of and communication with another dancer.

Here, then, for self-teachers and teachers of others are four Improvisational Rock Workshops as they evolved from 1975 to the present.

IMPROVISATIONAL ROCK DANCE WORKSHOP I

LESSON NO. 1

Each of the four Improvisational Rock Dance Workshops presented here consists of six one-hour lessons. Each lesson is divided into three parts: **Warmup, Lesson,** and **Free Dance.**

Warmup

The warmup involves *jogging, stretching,* and *isolated dancing.* Jogging to rock music is an unintimidating way to make that first scary move. Running is familiar and natural; it feels safe to run. So, I open each class with jogging to provide an outlet for nervous energy, to get our blood circulating rapidly with a greater supply of oxygen, to foster laughter, and to break through. In Lesson No. 1 I played "Break on Through" by The Doors.*

Every class tries to jog in circle formation. From the start I encourage students to improvise. "You may not run in a line," I call. "You do not have to follow anybody." They always giggle as they begin running helter skelter,

---

* Complete Music Index for all workshops listed elsewhere.

nearly bumping into each other. Soon my own jog evolves
to an outlandish set of movements. I extend arms, wiggle
hips, even run backwards. I am never too wild at first
though. Rather than overwhelm anyone, I mean only to
exemplify alternative choices of movement. Others, too,
become looser then, listen to the music better, and respond with unique movements, all in the name of jogging.

"Keep breathing!" I call. I dance through every lesson,
offering myself as model. My improvisations convey the
message that they, too, may give themselves permission to
move outrageously.

After the jog we form a circle and I lead the stretch
dance. I choose Blues. In the first workshop, and often
later, I used the excellent "Never Say No" by the Butterfield Blues Band. The stretch should be a flowing dance,
slow and smooth, thorough and continuous, with one
stretch being connected to the next. I use the same routine
each time. I like circles because they represent wholeness
and foster connecting. Briefly, the pattern is as follows:
we make circles slowly with our heads, then from our
chests and, finally, waists. With arms we draw a large circle
before us, bending and stretching completely. Then we
bring our arms to a circle around our bodies, twisting our
waists, feeling as if we are moving in slow motion under-
water. We do a variety of leg and feet stretches. Finally,
we do isometrics of the hands, fanny, and face. I encourage students to mug and grimace. "Make faces; be ugly. Do
not aim for glamour in this course. This class is a safe place.
Try new movement. We do not care how we look." Heavy
stuff, for no one wants to appear un-pretty. Giggling
self-consciously we make faces at each other. Occasionally
I permit students to create their own stretch dances. This
is meaningful for some, but too unstructured for others.
Of course teachers may vary the stretch dance to suit their
own class needs.

In the early Workshops, after the stretch we had a little

stompin' jam session to "Walking' Blues" by the Butterfield Blues Band. Stomping is an additional freeing device.
It allows women to release tight bodies and emotions, to
vary movement styles, and to transcend lady-like self
images. In short, stomping helps us "get down." Stomping
is the act of pushing the ball of the foot into the ground.
We created a simple pattern of striking twice with each
foot. "Smack that floor!" I would call. And with ticklish
delight we witnessed each other beginning to let go.

From the beginning to the end of every class I am
heard saying "Listen, really *listen*, to the music!" The
major block to one's dancing with ease and confidence is
her failure to hear the music. We are compelled by the
basic beat but hear none of the nuances. Consequently,
our dance often becomes as boring as that repetitious,
unrelenting throb — boom, boom, boom, boom. If one
listens *before* moving she will become acquainted with
the subtleties of all the instruments. Those subtleties provide motivation for a varied, interesting dance. She will
hear the "suspended" as well as the "ended" sounds. She
will move in a flowing (suspended) manner to the flute
perhaps, whereas she may do a more accented (ended)
movement in accompaniment to a drum. An enlarged
repertoire of movement comes with practice in listening.

Another important aspect of listening well is that of
letting the music come to the dancer. An inexperienced
dancer scarcely hears the first measure before charging to
the dance floor, only to rush past the music. There is not
even a clumsy collision; rather, a complete miss. Then her
dance feels disjointed and disconnected with everything,
including the music, her partner (if there is one), the space
and herself. I say to my students, "Listen first. Hear the
contrast of rhythms between the instruments, hear the variety of nuances, feel the overall mood. *Let the music
come to you.* Let it settle about your body, let it slip into
your pores. Become saturated with it. And when you have

merged with the music to *become* the music you will be ready to begin moving. At that point you will not have to think about it. By then, the music and your body, which are one, will do their own work, and your mind, like a third self, will watch with interest, participate without coercion.

"The process may begin with your swaying a bit. Maybe your hands and head will dance. If you are allowing yourself to tune in, at a precise moment you will be pleasantly surprised as the music carries you forward. From then on your body increases its movement steadily to the joyous completion of a total-body full-energy rock dance."

So, in the early days of the Workshops, after the stomping we had a listening session. I would play The Doors' "Light My Fire." To facilitate the music entering our bodies, we would breathe it in and out in eight counts in time with the song. Also, the students chose two instruments on which to concentrate, noting how they complemented one another.

The third part of the warmup is isolated dancing. (I explain isolated dancing in great detail in Workshop III.) From Workshop II through the evolution of the classes to the present, I have used the isolated dancing strictly in the warmup section. But in this first Workshop, which I taught for a year, I incorporated the isolated dancing into the *lesson* part of each session. (Some teachers may prefer this technique.) I used isolated dancing in this fashion for so long because the most important act involved in moving improvisationally is that of *allowing the music to come into the body*. Working with one body part at a time facilitates this act, increases concentration, and enlarges movement.

Lesson

During the Warmup, the students had allowed the music to enter their bodies by way of serious listening. Now they were to release the music, first only through their hands. I played "Tales of Brave Ulysses" by the rock group, Cream. Once again I served as model for them. They were free to imitate my movements and combine them with their own. I danced my hands with a variety of qualities (characteristics): high, low, smooth, sharp. They were encouraged to do the same. After experimenting with hands we let them rest and centered the movement initiative in the arms. I talked them through the isolated dancing, suggesting and explaining. "Lead with your elbows," or "watch that lazy upper arm. Give the energy to your shoulders alone now." I played a slow number, "We're Going Wrong," and told them to close their eyes and dance with their heads. Still using Cream's record we combined hands, arms, shoulders and head. They changed mood, force, quality, and level as the music demanded. I explained that with concentration their movements would evolve automatically to new movement. (More details on this kinesthetic principle in Workshop III.)

Continuing with isolated dancing we did hips and torso (the area between the neck and waist) to Cream's slow "Blue Condition." We worked the hips thoroughly, moving them in a complete circle, back and forth, and side to side. Regarding the torso, the part hardest to isolate, I would say, "think rib cage," from which the impetus for movement must come.

For an added challenge I changed the music to *The Virtuoso Recorder* by Bernard Krainis. We danced legs, then feet, to Vivaldi's Concerto in C Major. One at a time, I added shoulders, hips, torso, until the whole body danced. It was difficult dancing to Vivaldi but the students learned to listen harder and concentrate more intensely.

Free Dance

For the final portion of each session I encourage students to "let go." After struggling with Vivaldi, sliding into Fleetwood Mac's "Station Man" was easy. Once again I cautioned them to stand still and listen, letting the music travel to them. After it settled in, they moved just a little, gradually surrendering to it, trying both to remember and forget what they had just learned.

The free dance period each time is important for maintaining the vision of why we are together, *to enjoy dancing*, not merely to copy the teacher's suggestions and movements. In dancing freely, the students are reminded that the responsibility for giving themselves permission to dance lies with them, not with me. Each woman possesses her own dance power. I do not intend ever to steal that power or let anyone inadvertently misplace it in my pockets, my hands, or my mouth.

LESSON NO. 2

Warmup

Again the lesson began with jogging. I used Russian folk instrumental music. We did our stretch dance to a recorder piece from the *Virtuoso Recorder*, side one. Then came a listening period. Teachers who agree that fostering increased concentration in listening is important no doubt will use a variety of listening exercises to achieve that end. One idea I used in the early days when I had use of a stereo with two large floor speakers was to have the dancers go from speaker to speaker concentrating on the different sounds coming from each one. The physical division made it easy to identify the contribution made by each instrument. We would discern the flowing-movement melody of the flute or guitar at one speaker. At the other, we might hear the drum beat or a lesser instrument filling in with a small contrasting sound. As the students listened I asked them to imagine how their feet, legs, or shoulders would move to the various instruments. Eventually, we moved, one body part at a time. This was our isolated dancing for this lesson.

Lesson

The purpose of this lesson was to develop an advanced relationship between sound and movement. I brought small instruments to class — shakers, bells, tambourines, drums. As good teachers we must provide many activities that remind us all of the joy of dancing. I started this leslon by handing out the instruments, turning on a Marshall Tucker record and saying "play." To appreciate why this bit of unstructured experimental time was not too scary is to understand the feeling of comfort in holding a prop. True, it might be likened to holding a life preserver in an ocean, but still, it is *something*. People feel secure holding on, like Linus to his blanket or a dancer to her partner's hand in a jitterbug or disco dance. The student was free to play the instrument and move as little or as much as she felt secure doing. Whatever the degree, she was coming in touch with her own innovations, moving to her self-emanating sense of choreography.

After dancing awhile to a conglomeration of instrumental and record sounds, the women placed their music makers on the floor near my seated self. I explained that I would play the instruments one at a time and they were to move when they heard sound, move as long as there was sound, and stop immediately when the sound ceased. I suggested the quality of their movements be determined by the variety and quality of the sounds they heard. Drum beats might be harsh and big or small and soft. Other sounds would be irregular. Some would be constant and repetitious. They might be abrupt and sharp or jangly with discord like the chain I would spill on the floor. They were to listen for sustained sound like that of the triangle and keep moving in an appropriate fashion until they heard the sound no longer. I played each instrument in various ways. Students always respond well to this activity because it is fun. Their ability to listen and respond becomes acute. I insist they move only when they hear something and in some classes I insist they move when they hear *anything*. Finally, they move even to the noise of my putting down one instrument and picking up the next.

Free Dance

The free dance was performed without instruments to Marshall Tucker's record, *Take The Highway*. I gave a last word of instruction regarding this lesson: "Remember the isolated dancing and get in touch with a body part *you* usually do not use when you dance. Really listen, and then let go." I joined them then, getting involved with my own dance. I avoided watching at that time particularly, so they could begin to experience the joy and fulfillment of dancing for themselves only.

LESSON NO. 3

The music in this lesson was an added challenge to the dancers because it was all classical, except for the free dance. My reason for using all classical was to help us "break on through" to another dimension of movement. We do not give ourselves permission to dance to symphonies by Mozart because the unspoken pressures of artistic protocol demand that classical music be reserved for those formally-trained students on whom society bestows the title of "dancer." This is ridiculous! From the start I call my students "dancers." I say, "We will move freely to *all* kinds of music and it does not matter how we appear to others."

Warmup

The jog and stretch dance were combined in this lesson and the music for them was "Kalinka." In this Russian folk music the rhythm alternates between fast/bouncy and slow/dramatic. We would jog to the fast part, stop and stretch when the slow balalaikas played. This was good practice in listening and changing movement moods suddenly.

Lesson

"Kalinka" was appropriate music because Lesson 3 was Isadora Duncan Day. Isadora, portrayed by Vanessa Redgrave in the movie of her life, danced to "Kalinka" when she was in Russia, where she had gone to open a school. Isadora Duncan was the first American to dance barefooted and in loose clothing. The woman today who uses dancing as a catalyst for expressing the self, for demonstrating a free-thinking personality, and for guiding the emergence of powerful self determination will appreciate Isadora's bold dance behavior at the turn of the century. She was a free dancer and a free spirit. She chose not to confine her personal life to a rigid pattern nor her dance to a restrictive form.

I wanted other women to experience freedom and flow

in their improvisational dancing and thought the spirit of Isadora would help me achieve this end. I showed her picture; her costume was a frothy Greek toga. We practiced the Isadora walk and used our arms in the way she had. I taught the polka or skip step she used in her dances and we practiced to Mozart's Symphony in G, first movement.

Finally, we donned togas and held veils and danced improvisationally as Isadora had. (Isadora Duncan did choreograph her dances for public performance but that aspect was not pertinent to the purpose of this lesson.) We danced to Mozart's Symphony in G, second movement, and to Beethoven's Sonata "Pathetique," and to some music by Scriabin, one of Isadora's favorite composers. The veils were props that facilitated our dancing improvisation. It is never as difficult to dance to classical music as one images it will be. I suggested the students assign emotions to the nuances and changes in the music as they heard them, then act out the emotions, that is, dance them.

Free Dance

I played some of the Butterfield Blues Band *East West* record, a great classic of another type. Coming to simpler rhythms after the dancing we had just done would be easy.

With the culmination of the first three lessons, the first half of the Improvisational Rock Dance Workshop ended. The emphasis during the first half had been on dancing alone to one's own improvisation. In the second part we would continue to develop this skill, but the emphasis would shift from dancing alone to including others in both our awareness and our movements.

LESSON NO. 4

Warmup

With Lesson 4 I introduced Latin Rock to this Workshop. Music for jog and stretch came from Santana's *Abraxas*, side one. In the isolated dance I used side two of this excellent record. I conducted the isolated dancing somewhat differently this time. We started with the hands as always and gave all our energy to each body part in turn — arms, torso, hips, head, shoulders, legs, feet — letting only that one part be alive with movement. However, in keeping with the aim of including others in our dance, half way through I asked half the class to watch. In a few minutes I reversed the roles of watchers and movers.

I believe the way to foster self-confidence, so important to the successful execution of improvisational dancing, is to allow people to experience being oogled in the safe atmosphere of a class. Other students experiencing the same fears are supportive and non-judgmental. The more often one dances before others, the increasingly more confident one becomes in believing her dance is publicly acceptable. With this knowledge there develops not only a trust in one's own dance judgment, but an increased self-respect in regard to one's basic worth and ability to make effective choices in many areas besides dance.

So we watched each other, nervously at first. In Lessons 5 and 6, the last two sessions, we did more watching, more confidence building.

Lesson

In the early days of teaching rock dance I found people tripping over their feet. They felt they needed specific steps and asked for them. For many women the transition from the structured foot patterns of the jitterbug or swing dances, in which one's partner held our hands allowing us to feel secure, to the totally unstructured improvised movements of rock dancing with no hand to hold was difficult. (As independence in other areas of our lives, too, has been difficult.) "If I may not hold on to my partner, at least give me a foot pattern to attach to," is what they meant when they asked for specific steps. The four-beat rhythm of rock or jazz demands different foot work than does boogie woogie's eight to the bar that some of us knew. So the lesson this time was "feet."

I always started out by emphasizing the fact that when they had practiced enough rock, the dance would emanate from their centers, that place from which all movement arises effortlessly; and they would forget about feet. "As a help-mate in the meanwhile I will give you some simple foot movements." I used Robin Trower's music for its easy beat. A basic step for four-beat rock music is two stomps with each foot. Again, the stomp is a brisk hitting forward of the ball of the foot to the floor. Left, two; right, two. Any variation of this simple pattern works. One step each foot, left right, left right. Or, nice for Latin rock, is three small stomps for each beat. Right left right, pause, left right left, pause, etc., with the accent on the first stomp each time. We practiced each of these steps, then combined and alternated them.

Free Dance

Again we used Santana. First we all danced, then half of us, two at a time next, and finally, only one. Then we danced all together again, relieved to be lost in the group once more where we were sure noone watched us directly. We had stretched our self-confidence a bit and, as with a worked muscle, continual practice would allow it to grow in strength and endurance.

LESSON NO. 5

In Lesson 5 we got into African music and dance movements. I used African music for its variety of rhythm. (In retrospect I believe I was reaching back as far as I could to the beginning of dance rhythm as we know it in blues, jazz, and rock, all of these the same, a different name for a different time.)

Warmup

We began with a series of shaking and loosening exercises. I wanted to get the muscles and joints as relaxed, flexible, and lubricated as possible. Of course we jogged first, which improved our circulation and oxygen supply. Following the jog we shook the tension from every body part. Still jogging in place we loosened our hips, shoulders, and hands until we bobbed like puppets on strings. We bent from the waist, dangling our heads and arms, and shook ourselves gently in this position. The flowing of extra blood to the neck, thyroid, and head prepared us for vigorous African movements.

Lesson

We performed a series of movement exercises based on African dance. First, I showed the women a few simple arm and pelvic movements. I used the record, *Drums of Africa*, music of western Africa. In this music one hears what we identify as Latin traces. These are comfortable and familiar for most students. We played with this music, practicing movements individually, forming no particular configuration. We tilted pelvics and flapped elbows, moving to drums, shuffling our feet, feeling a new kind of body coordination, getting centered in a new sort of music.

Then I played Congo tribal music from the record, *Face of Africa*. We formed a line and I suggested they let themselves become absorbed, trance-like, with the sounds. "Let the music come to you as usual. Let it center itself in you. Let that centering give rise to your movement and continue to repeat the movement until you feel captive to its hypnotic quality." When they seemed comfortable with this we all did the same movement, entering into a group trance, and we took turns leading by one person changing the movement when she desired to do so. There was no stopping or talking between changes.

In the next exercise of this series I told them each to invent a variety of new movements for a new dance. Using as reference, movements we had just performed, this was not as difficult to do as it sounds. The record used was *Drums of Passion*. Then we took turns moving in pairs to the same music, with the others watching. Finally, rounding out the series, we repeated the group trance dance, taking turns leading. *Drums of Passion*, an excellent record, again was used.

Free Dance

I played a variety of African music and reminded them to use all their body parts in moving to these rhythms. The records were *Ninth Son, The Best of Miriam Makeba, Face of Africa*.

LESSON NO. 6

Warmup

We jogged and stretch danced to music by Herbie Mann, Side A of his record, *Push Push*. Isolated dancing followed. (Reminder: I guide the reader through detailed isolated dancing in Workshop III Lesson 1.)

Lesson

The sixth and final lesson of the Improvisational Rock Dance Workshops always has been an overall review. In this first Lesson No. 6 we began with some concentrated listening to the Grateful Dead's *Mars Hotel* record, Side 2. I reminded the women to hear the contrast of instruments, to determine the dominant movement quality or mood, to let the music come to them. Through the first song we breathed with the music, facilitating our absorbing of the rhythm. In Cuts 2 and 3 I talked us through our dances. "Use your hips. Change to another body part. Give energy to two parts at once. Smile at each other. Dance into another's rhythm. Change the quality (mood) of your dance midway."

We drank some wine. We talked about ourselves and dance. Paper and pencils were available and I asked for feedback notes on the Workshop. In a relaxed, dance-party mood, we were ready for the free dance.

Free Dance

As I have stated, my original motivation for establishing an Improvisational Rock Dance Workshop was to bring myself together with other women who wanted to dance and to suggest to them ideas for dancing more confidently. My measure of success of the Workshop would be that when we came together for this last dance we would be more expanded, less timid, and more joyful than we had been six weeks prior. This occurred for nearly everyone. One woman related to the class a dancing incident at a public club. "A man asked me to dance. I was nervous but decided to try what we had been practicing in class. I moved my hips and hands and really got into the music. At the end of the dance he exploded: 'I've never seen anyone dance like that!' he said. 'I think I'm in love with you!' "

As the final gesture of the first Improvisational Rock Dance Workshop, we formed a circle and pressed the palms of our hands together for a moment of silent sharing in celebration of our communion in movement called dance.

IMPROVISATIONAL ROCK DANCE WORKSHOP II

I continue to make changes in the Rock Workshops, incorporating new ideas and altering old ones. In this context the reader will notice I have used past tense in explaining Workshop I. I do so as well in Workshops II and III. As I have implied throughout *Power To The Dancers!* the Workshops represent a process of growth and change. In describing Workshops I, II, and III I am speaking of past experiences. This fact does not invalidate those Workshops as useful lesson plans. It means, simply, that I continue to adopt other varieties of teaching activities and methods. If this book were to be written five years hence, there would be included probably another Workshop, a future product of evolution.

Therefore, in using this book teachers may try a complete workshop at one time; and, for another class, pick and choose to form a new series. Individual women improving their own dancing may do the same, alone or with friends.

LESSON NO. 1

Warmup

I vary music constantly because when one is forced to listen anew, she must improvise accordingly. For the jog and stretch of this warmup I used the *Prism Album* of the British rock group, Pink Floyd. Their unusual piece, "Money", with its challenges, provides much opportunity for movement changes. I asked the women to stretch, then jog, jog doubletime, and return to stretching movements, as the music demanded. They were instructed to treat this warmup series as if it were a complete dance, that is, to connect one activity with the next in a flowing movement creation. Though I provided guidance during this eight-minute jog-stretch warmup, the students were free to choreograph their own dances if they so chose.

The isolated dancing was performed to Cream's *Disraeli Gears* album, Side 2. As usual, we listened before moving. This time I approached isolated dancing differently. The women were told to sit on the floor. We would experience the feeling of dancing without standing. This activity emphasized the unimportance of steps in rock dancing. I led them through a seated dance of hands, arms, shoulders, torso, and head. To insure greater concentration we closed our eyes through part of the exercise.

Finally we stood to dance hips and legs. Purposely, I ignored feet in this warmup but did include, affectionately, fanny. We shook that lovely, loose fat, giving ourselves permission to let it dance, peeking over our shoulders to validate and glorify that beautiful part of our anatomy that we as proper ladies have had to pretend does not exist.

Lesson

It became more and more apparent to me that people in public dance places as well as students in my classes varied movement only slightly, if at all, when they danced improvisationally. They used the same tired gestures and repetitious steps. Force and intensity were never varied; rhythm stayed even; limited body was used. (Hip people always used hips; shoulder people, shoulders, etc.) In short, the mood of the dance was always predictably the same. I felt then, and still do, that the main reason people think they cannot dance well is that, unbeknown to themselves even, their own dances bore them. They have conditioned themselves to move a certain set way to rock music without understanding the subtle differences in qualities throughout the many categories of this music. To the experienced listening dancer each mood carries a unique suggestion for movement. Each kind of rock — country, jazz, hard, or space — invites one to dance a different way.

So I decided to help students identify qualities and move differently with each one. (I use the words "mood" and "quality" interchangeably.) I chose the Grateful Dead's *American Beauty* album. I assigned a one-word quality to each of four cuts on Side 1: Cut 2, "bounce," Cut 3, "swing," Cut 4, "sway," Cut 5, "circles." We listened to some of each song, visualizing the assigned qualities and differentiating between them. Then we worked on one at a time.

On Cut 2 I asked the women to feel their bodies bouncing gently, first feet, then knees. I told them to bring the bouncing sensation to their hips. "Feel like a puppet on strings. Bounce the music off your shoulders, torso, and head. Experience floppy letting go. Dangle your arms while you bounce, and bend your sides." When they seemed loose I said, "Now tune into the intricacies of the music and make your bouncing *active* instead of puppet passive. Now direct the bounce. Instead of dangling arms, hold them up, dancing them in the spaces around your body. Control the bounce while retaining flexibility and range of movement."

We treated each succeeding quality in the same fashion. Through Cut 3 I led the class in a basic swinging movement. We plunged forward with feet and arms for eight counts, then moved backwards for the next eight. Bending our bodies backward and forward, we went up eight, back eight. When the women had the feeling of the back and forth swing quality, I changed the count to four. Four up, four back. Then two. And, finally, one. By the time we reached one count each forward and back, the movement was a rocking one. At this point I told them to tune into the music and improvise rocking movements with various body parts. "Use arms, hands, hips. Retaining the music's style and rhythm, dance as you choose to, letting the swinging quality guide you. Keep coming back to it. Use it as inspiration for your dance creation."

We went on to "sway." Whereas swing travels forward and back, sway goes from side to side. I referred to isolating the rib cage, the place from which sway action emanates. When the rib cage reaches one side, the shoulders and head follow; and by the time they are there, the rib cage has begun its leading movement in the opposite direction. The resultant motion is like a whiplash or an undulation. This movement has a natural flow and takes practice to attain. I stand before the class with my back to them so they may copy my timing and flow. Soon we put the sway quality in our hips too. Variations of this movement are possible, from a quick, snappy side to side rhythm to a long undulating gesture like a wave.

Once again we improvised. "As you did with the swing,

let the sway take you in any direction at any speed. Feel like hula hands throughout your body. Use that feeling as the basis for your dance." As with any activity, success demands practice. I always suggest women practice dancing at home.

The last quality was "circles." Cut 5 is slow, offering possibilities for expanded dance. "Think roundness and fullness. Capture as much space as you can reach. Expand the very atoms of your bodies and form circles with them. Take advantage of the roominess of this place to experience yourself in space." I directed them to dance large, sweeping movements into open areas of the huge room, until, with ease, each woman discovered she could enlarge the space in which she functioned. If she could accomplish this in dance she could do it in the rest of her world as well.

People do not use arms enough in dancing. To illustrate the value of dancing arms I told the students to continue their expanded dance holding arms at their sides. It was difficult to do with arms inert. Balance was off; innovation, restricted. With their bodies thus inhibited, the room's opposite side seemed completely out of reach, like the pot of gold at rainbow's end. "Now reach out and grab again," I called. The dance resumed its effortless flow, like harnessed energy set free. This exercise demonstrated the potential of each woman's self-power.

Regarding the movement qualities, I emphasized that each dancer might hear a different quality than someone else hears in a piece of music. No one song need present the same quality to each person. With careful listening a dancer will perceive the individual quality best for her. Only for the purpose of class practice did we all use the same qualities. Listening to this music elsewhere a woman might hear an emotional quality of *sadness* instead of *sway* or *silliness* instead of *bounce*. Later, with practice, she will identify more than one mood in each song. At that point her ability to improvise will increase and dancing will become exciting.

Free Dance

In the short time left I played Pink Floyd again. I asked each person to listen for a quality and assigned it as the theme for her free dance.

LESSON NO. 2

The longer I teach, the more sure I become that people need to identify music "moods" in order to create satisfying dances. The people who claim they cannot dance and the others who look bored when they do are those who separate the music from themselves. The space between them and the music alienates one from the other. Music is the tool with which, if she learns to relate to it, a woman may raise her dancing consciousness. There are many ways we may learn to better appreciate that tool, to work through it, and to merge with it. In this lesson I concentrated on the contrasts within a piece of music and the variety of movements possible in regard to those contrasts.

Warmup

I used the record *Push Push* by Herbie Mann, a jazz flutist. Nearly every cut of this record represents highly contrasting sound qualities between the flute and drum. We translated those sounds into "sustained" and "sharp" movements in the isolated dancing. First the class tuned in to the drum and improvised a "sharp" dance with one body part. Then they switched their listening to the flute and let the same body part flow in a "sustained" dance. They were reminded to move for as long as they perceived the sound quality and to change when their perception changed.

Lesson

To give the women more practice with "sharp" and "sustained" contrasts, I played the bongo drums, then a triangle, asking them to respond to the sounds in staccato or flowing fashion. When they were clearly aware of definite alternating changes in their dances, I played *Inside* by Paul Horn, a recording of flute and chants inside India's Taj Mahal. This record consists of a series of short phrases by flute and voice with echoes and silences in between the phrases. The women were to move for as long as they heard music, and stop when it stopped, holding that body position until they began again with a new sound wave. We used whole bodies and a number of levels, from high space to the floor.

For the opposite extreme I played Taj Mahal's "Cakewalk," a banjo-pluckin' "git down and do it!" piece of music. This song is most conducive to dancing sharp and jerky. The first two cuts on Side 1 of Marshall Tucker's *Take The Highway* are also good. I followed these songs with flowing, sustained pieces: Nilsson's "Moonbeams" and "Sweet Fire" by Joni Mitchell. We recalled the "circles" quality of the preceding lesson, expanding ourselves to flow into space.

Free Dance

I played more of Herbie Mann's *Push Push* with its alternations between sustained and sharp. Before beginning

I suggested three guides for this free dance period: Do what the music commands, think about quality, and dance a new body part. Once again then, I left them to experience privately their rising ability to extemporize while I enjoyed my own dance.

LESSON NO. 3

As in Workshop I, this Lesson No. 3 also was devoted to the flowing style of Isadora Duncan, with modification. That is, we used the veils to further our work in "suspended" and "ended" rock dance movements. With a sense of indebtedness to Isadora Duncan's influence, I felt compelled to teach women about her. The women taking my classes have been ones most anxious to be opened to dance. Isadora was the perfect model. In all the Improvisational Rock Workshops following this one, however, though I continued to talk about Isadora, I stopped devoting an entire lesson to her. (Teachers desiring a modified Isadora Duncan lesson may prefer this one to that of Workshop I.)

Warmup

I used the same warmup music, "Kalinka," in the fashion described in Workshop I Lesson 3, that is, alternating jogging and stretching.

Lesson

I used classical music as before to teach the Isadora Duncan style. We did not wear togas but we did dance holding veils. I told the students to sense particularly the quality of "flow" in using the veils. After guiding them through Isadora's classical music we changed to a flowing rock song, "Do You Feel as We Do?" by Peter Frampton on the record, *Camel.*

"Do You Feel?" is a piece I have used often in class-work for its valuable rhythm changes. The song begins with one electric guitar delivering an earthy phrase that is repeated often throughout, a soulful phrase that reaches out and envelops the dancer. One does not resist. Immediately it is repeated with other instruments giving it depth, and with the drum giving it contrast. From here on the dancer is tempted first by the beseeching undercurrent of the drum beat's rhythm and then by the sensual beckoning of its contrast, the strings and voices. I call the mood "heavy molasses." Movement feels like a movie in slow motion. When the voices begin the verses, repeating the melodic, "do you feel as we do?" it is obvious the feeling is spacey and one dances accordingly.

So far the class has danced smoothly to this piece, flowing with arms into space. Now there is a change. The voices stop. All instruments play a brisker dance. "Change your quality to sharpness now. Be less concerned with traveling through space. Limit your dance to concentrated body movements." When the lead guitar improvises, I say, "Hear it with your body, not your ears. Let your body and the guitar's music become joined and move as one."

Before beginning I had alerted the women to three conditions: 1) the lead guitar's individual improvised song, 2) the drum's steady beat, 3) all other instruments drawing them into a syrupy flow dance. We danced the rest of the piece with my directing them in and out of "suspended" and "ended" movements to a finale of highly interpretive instrumental sounds which made for extremely creative dancing.

To enhance the feeling of flow in this seven-minute song we used the veils some of the time. As in the Isadora dances, veils supplemented one's sense of smooth motion. And with the achievement of this essential task, one brings herself not only further into meaningful dance but closer to a sense of harmony between other aspects of her life as well.

Free Dance

The class relaxed with Nilsson's "Moonbeams," heeding my instructions to rest from the intensive listening work of this lesson and dance loosely and meditatively. I did the same.

LESSON NO. 4

Warmup

Occasionally during my early days of teaching I allowed the warmup to be wholly unstructured, especially in the second half of the workshop. By then students were becoming comfortable with their bodies. An unstructured warmup let them take responsibility for deciding how to move. "Just dance," I would say and play good old rock and roll, like the Beatles' *Sergeant Pepper* album or Edgar Winter's song, "Rock and Roll Woman." Their dancing spontaneously related to this lesson's theme: *pure improvisation in dance movement*. Exactly what is it? When does it occur? How does one arrive at a successful improvisational dance?

Lesson

We started with discussion of what movement improvisation is, based on the concepts of Gay Cheney and Janet Strader in their book, *Modern Dance*. These concepts are discussed in another section of this book, but they bear reviewing. There are three main facts to consider: 1) Improvisational dance is purely kinesthetic in that there is no preplan or choreography involved. 2) One movement necessarily leads to another. 3) One must attain the state of being "in" to have a successful improvisation.

"In" is a state in which the dancer concentrates fully on the present moment of the improvisation. She is aware of her surroundings but is more involved with what is happening in the dance. Her concern is with the dance and her focus is on the evolution of the movement. In a way, she is a curious bystander to an automatic dance. And yet she must not be mentally on the outskirts of the action. Body and mind must function at the same instant.

How does she get "in"? First of all, she must forget herself. Besides focusing on the movement, she may concentrate on another dancer, the music, or on any other part of the dance but herself. She must allow herself to be drawn into the spirit of the dance. She must tune in to the dominant quality of the extemporaneous moment. I stress careful listening to the music so she may relinquish herself fully to the mood and flow of the dance. At the end of a dance, when she "awakens" from an absorbed state, she will know she had reached the blissful state of "in." With practice this condition becomes easier to attain.

There is *structured* and *free* improvisation. In the Warmup and Free Dance portions of each lesson we perform much *free* improvisation. Now we would do two *structured* improvisation exercises, one individual and one group. For the individual task we used a straight-backed chair and music by Bach played by guitarist Christopher Parkening. In some classes each dancer had a chair and we perfomed the exercise all at once, thankful for the privacy and anonymity of a group. In other classes we watched one person at a time. I always performed first alone to break the ice for this difficult challenge.

The instructions for this improvisation were as follows: "Focus on nothing but the music and the chair. See the chair's lines. Think how you will shape your moving body to the chair's size and bulk. Influenced by the music's mood, move in and around the chair. Is the chair static and unrelenting? Or smooth and easy? Reflect its character in the shapes of your dance. You may wish to move in symmetrical designs, for instance." (In one class we had an over-stuffed chair and the dancers' movements were soft and round as a result.) "Do not plan the dance ahead of time. Strive for letting go and falling 'in.' "

The second improvisation involved the group. We made a group shape to begin, each person touching another in bent, straight, or twisted positions. I played Side 1, Cut 2 from *The Sounds of India* by Ravi Shankar. "Develop a sense of the group quality or mood," I said. The dance that resulted would be perfectly right, whether it was meager or elaborate. "One movement will flow to another and bring you along with it, if you allow it without forcing." A group dance is scary and exciting and does not always work the first time, but with practice it becomes easier to do. The feeling of personal fulfillment is most rewarding.

Free Dance

Now it was time to relax into rock. I played Country Joe and said to focus on the variations in the music, to forget the structured exercise and simply freely improvise.

LESSON NO. 5

In this lesson I introduced basic African dance movements, as I had done in Lesson 5 of the first Workshop. In addition, we worked on "beat" exercises because students had trouble with the rhythm of rock music. Trance-like African movements are similar in mood to the simple four-beat rock rhythm. I felt the practice of the former would facilitate the performance of the latter.

Warmup

Again, in addition to the regular jogging period, we shook our limbs and bounced lightly like puppets to loosen joints and flex muscles. We extended our arms overhead, stretched high, then collapsed suddenly to the floor, immediately straightening legs while leaving our upper body dangling over from the waist. Very slowly we arose one vertebra at a time, with head being last up.

Lesson

I used my favorite African record, *Drums of Passion* by Olatumi. First we performed some of the African dance exercises described previously. (Refer to Workshop I Lesson 5.)

In the "beat" part of the lesson I asked the women to create a simple two-gesture pattern of four beats. For instance, clap clap, stamp stamp. Or, finger snap snap, hands clap clap. One, two — three, four. When they could do this easily they chose partners and taught each other their routines. When the couples knew each routine well I introduced the music "White Sugar," from Peter Frampton's *Camel* record, which I chose for its simplicity of beat. Each person practiced her own routine to the music, and that of her partner, until she felt comfortable with the rhythm and both patterns. Next, facing one another, the partners took turns leading each other at will through their respective dance patterns. The goal of this part of the exercise was to keep the rhythm flowing from change to change, from woman to woman, without missing a beat, or at least catching up quickly if they did momentarily slack in the flow.

Free Dance

We took this time to explore privately rock's simple four-beat rhythm and further familiarize ourselves with it. I played "White Sugar" again as the women internalized, through their individual dances, the feeling of one, two — three, four.

LESSON NO. 6

Warmup

The Warmup had been evolving through the past lessons to the set, solid format used in this lesson. It has remained constant in the succeeding Rock Workshops, as well as the Creative Dance Workshop classes, as follows: five minutes of jogging, a group circle stretch dance, and a period of isolated dancing.

Lesson

We reviewed briefly the lesson of each of the past five weeks. First, we practiced "quality." I played Herbie Mann's song "Push Push" from the album of the same name. We danced first to the flowing flute, then changed to reflect earthier drum beats. Following this, we worked on "beat" a bit, stomping and counting through Frampton's "White Sugar." For practice in isolations I played some of each from Janis Joplin's *Kosmic Blues* record and Cream's *Disraeli Gears*. "Dance to these as you feel them, but pay particular attention to moving different parts of your bodies in new ways." Finally, we used veils, bouncing playfully with them in improvisational dance to the Beatles' "When I'm 64" and "Rita Meter Maid" from the *Sergeant Pepper* album.

Free Dance

"The only instruction for our last dance together is to remember dancing is joyful," I said, directing half the class to dance and half to watch. "Have fun; know you are being watched but know, too, that that does not matter. You dance for your own enjoyment only, and every step and gesture you make is correct." The second half danced then, as the first group watched. Ideally, each person had gained self-confidence during the six weeks. I suspected dancing before the teacher and half the class was less painful than it would have been on our first meeting. I was sure that with continued practice each woman would come to appreciate fully her individual movement style and accept it as the perfect way for her to dance.

IMPROVISATIONAL ROCK DANCE WORKSHOP III

LESSON NO. 1

Warmup

We jogged to a fast piece on the highly electric record,

Blow by Blow by Jeff Beck and stretched to the slower " 'Cause We've Ended as Lovers." on the same record. Still in a circle we began the isolated dancing. For many reasons I consider the isolated dancing period to be the crucial part of every lesson. First, it liberates the body physically. What is more, it is the most valuable structured activity I use for teaching improvisation. The students are more readily inclined to experiment when they are directed to confine movement to one body area only. The isolated dancing routine I use presently in all classes originated in this Rock Workshop III. I describe it thoroughly in the paragraphs that follow.

We always begin with hands. At first the students dance hands cautiously in the area directly in front of their bodies to the music's basic beat. Their movements are limited. Gradually they expand their dances as they respond to suggestions. "Change your level," I may say. "Reach into the space above your head." Or, "Let one hand dance to the side of you while the other wanders into forward space. Put vitality into the hands. Extend fingers with strong gestures. Soften to hula hands. Make sweeping motions; intercept with little jabs. Be tuned in to the music; let it guide you with its own suggestions."

We give energy to arms next. The hands simply follow; the shoulders wait quietly. The dancer's consciousness is in her arms. Here I may speak of quality or mood. "Elbows do a jerky dance. Upper arms have their own strength. Release the arms in exploration; recall them back then, close to home." When concentration is centered on one dancing body part alone that part becomes stronger, more flexible and more versatile. Dancing becomes more interesting for the dancer as she accepts the challenge to improvise which leads to an enlarged movement repertoire. She discovers her dancing needs are more fully satisfied by improvising and learns that each new innovation leads to another and another, excitingly forward.

Shoulders next. "Tread lightly here," I say. "The muscles and nerves through the shoulders and neck shield worries and concerns, transforming them to knots of tension and soreness. Cajole the shoulders with gentle, smooth moves until you feel them relax. Gradually bring intricacy to their movement. Perhaps one shoulder at a time may dance. Or shimmy as in a rumba." Acute awareness and concentration at all times is necessary for isolated dancing to benefit the student. The women may not talk to one another, rather they must listen more attentively to the music.

When a slow piece plays I tell them to close their eyes and dance into their heads. I suggest slow circles at first, relaxing and breathing into neck tension, feeling it dissolve. "Let yourself and the music become one." Closing their eyes eliminates distraction and self-consciousness. Being in commune with the music allows one to flow unhampered.

Torso is the next body part we isolate. The torso is the area between the neck and waist. It is the most difficult part of the body to isolate. "Think rib cage," I say. "Move the rib cage from side to side. In your mind's eye picture your upper body sliding across your hips. Now picture it protruding forward and back." Often it takes students several sessions to move this part with ease and then dance it with rhythm. But finally movement consciousness of this area is established and muscles are strengthened.

We move on to the hips. Though women are in touch with their hips already, even here dance innovation becomes stagnant. I instruct them to dance the hips in a full circle — left, back, right, front — and not cheat at any corner. After this practice we tip the pelvic forward and back and finally diagonally as in a belly dance. Hip work is hard work. The women find that though they may readily wiggle their hips in dancing, to vary that movement means developing stronger muscles. Furthermore, to dance more excitingly means developing methods of improvisation.

"For instance," I call, "don't take the easy way with hips. Instead of simply keeping predictable drum-beat time, tune in to a slower, more melodic instrument and draw its musical pictures with your hips."

Legs are next, a great challenge because the balls of one's feet must remain rooted in the floor. To supply energy to the legs alone is to experience a lesson in expanded body awareness. We use our legs for support and guidance, not for creating. Unfortunately, we seldom apply improvisational powers to a "legs" dance. But when we do, as in class, they light up, to our pleasant surprise, as if they had been touched with a magic wand. In fact, our bodies sparkle all over when we dance all parts, feeling better balanced and more evenly used.

At first movement of the legs is limited. I see slight panic in the students' faces. "Legs alone?! And rooted yet?" But progressively each dancer develops flexible, creative legs. By resting over-worked parts, like hips, we have channeled dance to dormant areas.

Finally, feet. "Let your body be a zombie while your feet take off and fly!" I remind the women to heed the music and their feet *only*, turning off the rest of the body. "How do your feet contact the floor? Alternate between placing them lightly and heavily. Dance on one foot. Do something with your feet that you have never done before. Be silly. Have fun." I repeat that this is a safe place to try something new. "This is a place to laugh with yourself and to take yourself seriously and not so seriously, which is a very healthy thing to do."

Lesson

Once again the lesson dealt with "quality" but in a different way. I used the Grateful Dead's *American Beauty* album again. I described the same basic qualities:

"bounce," "swing," "sway," "circles," as found in Workshop II Lesson 1. After we had worked sufficiently with these qualities I played rock pieces at random and told the women to choose words for them. We danced to the words. I started with "funky." Among others, some of the qualities named were "jungle," "jazzy," "sensuous," "joyful," "hot," and "cool." We spent a very short time dancing each one. It was fun to change dance moods, like acting out. Particularly, it was beneficial for us to witness the growth of our dancing versatility.

Free Dance

Because of this lesson's length, often there was only five dancing minutes left to "relax and let go."

LESSON NO. 2

In this lesson I confront "beat" again, in a different manner still. (For other work with "beat" the reader may refer to Workshop I Lesson 4 and the African section of Workshop II Lesson 5.) Here we fashion irregular dances based on stopping our rhythm and movement suddenly, doing a split-second recentering of ourselves, and continuing on renewed.

Warmup

After our jog and stretch period, as usual we swung into isolated dancing. We danced each body part separately, alternating qualities and changing rhythms. When we had finished the last part, the feet, I "danced them up." That is, I reawakened each body part, starting with feet, with a directive to dance. "Dance your legs now, still delivering energy to your feet as well." In a while I added hips. "Now, torso. Altogether, feet, legs, hips, torso. The rest of your body should be holding in abeyance. Feel the dance energy in only those parts I have called so far." Then we continued. "Add shoulders; add arms." Et cetera, until the entire body rocked, according to Janis Joplin, "in a full-tilt boogie!"

Lesson

From full-tilt we moved to the Pointer Sisters' "Betcha' Got a Chick on the Side" from the album, *Steppin'*. This funky piece is perfect for exaggerated stop and go movements. I used it in this context in several ways. I divided the phrases into eight beats. I would count one, two, three, four, five, six, *stop*. For those last two beats, seven and eight, the women were to make a very quick accented stop. First we walked the six and held for two. I emphasized that "stop" was the highlight of the phrase. So the walk must build with vigor to the cherry on the top, not melt into it like ice cream.

After the women got the feel of this we danced two sharp movements for six counts and held for two. These movements were simple ones repeated — for instance, elbows and hips jab out, or arms and knees bend. At this point the movements were not important. The stop was. During the stop, in the space of two short counts, I expected them to pull it all together and begin again. Each time the stop represented a mini renewal of their dances in progress.

For the next part of the exercise I changed the quality of the movement. The stop remained the same, *two counts of sharp stillness*. Now they made one flowing gesture for six beats, a gesture that built to the stop. When they came out of the stop, they began the next flowing gesture from the position at which they had left off. Again, the stop was the highlight.

Finally, they were to do *any* improvisational movement for six counts, stop for two, renew, and start again. Needless to say, with this music the quality of the exercise was "funky."

I reminded the women that this stop gimmick is an improvisational tool that can be used with any music in every dance they perform. It is helpful especially when one feels stale in the dance, either with the music or the beat. Stop for a second, catch the quality again, and begin anew.

Free Dance

I played some of Janis Joplin's full-tilt boogie music from the album, *Kosmic Blues*. I told them to practice stopping and to have fun playing "funky."

LESSON NO. 3

In my mind I referred to this lesson always as the "cultural" one. I felt exposure to music from other countries would not only broaden our experience with varying rhythms, making us appreciative of the simplicity of our own rock beat, but it would furnish a fresh opportunity for practicing improvisation. Therefore, I brought the music of other cultures to the original African lesson. I did not know the dances of all these countries. That did not matter. To assimilate the rhythms with our bodies *was* what was important.

Warmup

For the jog, stretch, and isolated dancing "Kalinka" seemed appropriate. The reader must remember the Workshops evolved gradually and constantly, a situation I found delightfully renewing. Each Workshop in time relinquished itself gracefully to its successor. In this manner the Isadora lesson faded from my use. "Kalinka" was all that was left, and I used it in this warmup as a tribute to the woman whose style inspired me to grow in dance and in life.

Lesson

We started in central Africa. Our bodies blended with the hypnotic drums of the Congo. We practiced movements in rhythmic repetition. (See Music Index for Workshop I for complete African list.) I played western African music next with its undercurrent of samba sounds. The women tuned in with familiarity. Some found the music possessing their shoulders. Others exorcised it through their hips. We continued with northern Africa, where the exotic presence of ancient Egyptian music mingles with middle-eastern sensuousness. With drums, flutes, bells, cymbals, the music is repetitive and ritualistic. "Listen and feel how it differs from that of western Africa. Be aware of how this music affects your personal rhythm and how you change to accommodate that new feeling. In what part of your body does this new rhythm center?"

Then, to the tip of north Africa and Tunisian music, which differs slightly from that with an Egyptian influence but also is heavily middle eastern. Across the Mediterranean Sea into Romania. With eastern European folk music our rhythm changes again. Because the beat is similar to that of our American folk dances, we find this music familiar. The dance centers in our feet as we heed the urge to heel and toe and stomp stomp stomp. I instructed the women to abandon their bodies intuitively to the sound.* We arrived at the waltz. The waltz is a simple three-beat step, easy to learn and resembling the polka, which we had just done with the folk dance music. I encouraged the women to release themselves to a swooping-waltz feeling. "Think of Vienna!"

Finally, we were ready to return to rock. The ethnic sounds of *Primal Roots* by Sergio Mendes, with its roots in jazz, carried us back quickly to our own culture's popular music.

Free Dance

We rocked out to Side 1 of Janis Joplin's *Kosmic Blues*. Its familiar beat, after three foreign continents, allowed us to improvise with ease.

LESSON NO. 4

This lesson dealt directly with improvisation again. We discussed the nature of movement improvisation and did practice exercises which were different than those performed in preceding classes.

Warmup

I used the record *Love Man* by the late Otis Redding. We jogged and then stretched to slower blues. As we began

---

*   In addition to my own records, I use those of the local library. I suggest teachers and individuals explore the wide selection of records available for loan at many city libraries.

isolated dancing I encouraged them to remember and use improvisational "gimmicks" like the stopping technique we practiced with the Pointer Sisters record. "Combine the stops with changing rhythms and alternating qualities," I suggested. "And use as much space as you can reach."

Lesson

I had emphasized the importance of feeling "in" during an improvisation exercise. (Workshop II Lesson 4.) A reminder: being "in" is the condition in which a dancer's total consciousness is focused on the movement. The other two guidelines for improvisational dance are equally important and they too require understanding. The first is that *improvisational movement is purely kinesthetic*; that is, there is no preplan or choreography. This is a difficult principle to apply in practice. One must become *unself-conscious*. Therefore, I supplied something to distract the women's attention from themselves. Each person was given a small musical instrument to dance with — a shaker, tambourine, hand drum, or sticks. I selected *Primal Roots*, Sergio Mendes' Brazil '77. "Listen to the music and look at your instrument while you dance. I do not care what your body does. Do not strive for versatility, expansiveness, or any other movement trait. Absolutely do not think about what you are dancing. Become hypnotized by your instrument and the music." They tended to check in and out of self-consciousness. As a result, their dances were excitingly spontaneous in part. The twinkling of discovery flashed on faces when they had finished.

The second principle of improvisation is that *one movement necessarily leads to the next*. When a dancer forgets her mental and emotional self finally, like switching to automatic, her body takes over. When she relin-

quishes the idea of controlling her dance by choreograph-
ing it, new things happen. For as her body becomes bored
ultimately with the same tired movements of her style, it
will automatically create new dance. I illustrated the vali-
dity of this principle in a simple, physical way. They made
a circle and I walked in and out of it, looking into their
faces and finally stopping before one woman to ask her
to walk with me. There was no music. We held hands. The
walking became exaggerated and developed into a swinging skip. Neither of us directed the movement. It had
changed subtly, evolving to something else according to
our personalities. I brought her back to the circle and proceeded to another woman.

The encounters in this exercise always differ. Most of
the time the circle remains in tact with each person waiting
anxiously for her turn. In some classes a third person joins
the walking. Sometimes the spirit or momentum of the
walkers causes other to touch them or to begin their own
walk.

Free Dance

Having just experienced the kinesthetic principle that
one movement leads to another, the class now could observe this phenomenon in their free rock dancing period.
Creedence Clearwater's famous "Suzie Q," which plays for
eight and a half minutes, has a hypnotic, repetitive quality.
The women allowed themselves to be mesmerized by the
music, to move automatically. At the end, we discussed
the evolution of their individual dances.

LESSON NO. 5

Warmup

We jogged, stretched, and danced in isolation to the Butterfield Blues Band, Janis Joplin, and the Quicksilver Messenger Service, one of San Francisco's early rock bands. "Obey the music. But do not wear yourself out chasing a bumpy beat. Use the short stops for mini renewals of energy and spirit. Remember, too, you may move smoothly and slowly in contrast to the basic beat." I wanted the students to value meditation in dance, that slow, continuous movement which puts one in complete touch with her dance and her body in space.

The music is a guide and companion, not an adversary to be overcome. The women were to receive its power and combine it with their own to produce a full-energy dance. "Work *with* the music," I said. "Work *with* the rhythm. Work *with* the changing qualities."

Lesson

At the time of this lesson a revival of the swing era was taking place, with its big-band sound of the 40s. With it came the jitterbug, that dance of discovery for me at age twelve. There it was again, the dance I had sharpened my shoes on, fancy-stepped through adolescence with, and forever used as a tool for raising my self-esteem. Women wanted to learn it. How could I refuse? I did not try. So, I taught them the jitterbug even though it is a dance of choreographed footwork instead of improvisational movement. I taught it for two good reasons. First, it furnished structure for those women still insecure with unstructured dances. After all, they had had only five weeks of freedom out of a lifetime of "bound feet." Secondly, this dance was a reward after they had worked so hard on unstructured movement, a measure against which they could perceive their increasing self-confidence and creative skill. When a person has completed a difficult task, by comparison the easier one that follows proves her competence. She owns her power.

So, we jitterbugged. The beat is 6/8, and I break it down to *one and two and three and*. The footwork: Right left, left right, right left, and start over again with right. The last "right left" is a bit of a hop, a mere shifting of weight. The pattern: With feet together the right foot steps forward and to the side (diagonally.) The left comes up to meet it. That is *one and*. Next, the left returns to its original place and the right follows. Now they are in the original position. That is *two and*. The right goes back and to the side (diagonally) and the left steps in place. That is *three and*. Repeat from the top. That is all. The pattern is repeated again and again, even as the dancers turn and move about. The partners hold one hand each, sometimes two.

There is one point of which to be aware — the position of the feet on the *three and*. They are not together, as in the beginning. So all the succeeding *one ands* begin with the right foot coming from the back position.

The jitterbug footwork is simple. A mental visualization of the pattern would be an arrowhead with the left foot forever the apex. Good music to use is that with a boogie woogie beat from the 40s and rock and roll from the 50s. Libraries are a source for records of this type, as are used record stores.

Free Dance

We continued practicing the jitterbug, mostly alone.

Some caught on quickly and tried partners. Sometimes women discovered jitterbugging was not what they had wanted after all. Secretly this pleased me. For I maintain that once one has trusted herself to improvise, to test her power to dance and live freely, the need for an iron-clad, prescribed pattern vanishes.

LESSON NO. 6

As in other Workshops, the last lesson of this one was a review of what we had learned in order to measure the growing confidence in ourselves to create innovative rock dances. However, this review differed from past ones.

Warmup

We jogged and stretched as usual. I used the Jefferson Airplane's *Surrealistic Pillow*, an early classic rock album. For the isolated dancing I used "Creeque Alley" from *The Mamas and Papas Deliver*, a danceable tune blending hard beat and smooth flow.

Lesson

The musical, *Hair*, that pioneer of rock music in stage-play form, seemed appropriate for our budding improvisational talents. What could be more inspiring than dancing to show numbers. We danced nine short pieces. I told them the name of each dance and a bit about it. I assigned a quality to each song. The album is the RCA recording with the original Broadway cast, *Hair: The American Tribal Love Rock Musical*. (Very 60s.) As they ended each dance and before they began the next, I reminded them of the upcoming quality. Here, then, are the nine numbers and the assigned qualities or moods: 1) "Aquarius." A rock hymn in which the Tribe mystically calls forth its visions of harmony and understanding. (Notes from album jacket.) Quality: *flowing.* 2) "Donna." Quality: the opposite, *jerky.* 3) "Sodomy." Quality: *slow spoof.* This dance was to be one continuous movement. 4) "Colored Spade." Quality: *cool.* 5) "Manchester, England." Quality: *polka* (three beats) 6) "I'm Black" and "Ain't Got No." Quality: *Afro-waltz* (Also three beats.) Numbers 5 and 6 provided excellent opportunity to vary a three-beat dance. 7) "Air." Quality: *two-step.* 8) "Initials." Quality: *minuet parody.* 9) "I Got Life." A defiant, proud, and joyous theme (jacket notes.) For No. 9 I wanted the women to express this description in their dances, so I assigned the quality of *open joy.*

Free Dance

Hair was daring and new when first produced, challenging a stereotype society. I told the students that their spirits should be no less daring in challenging dancing that was stereotyped and dull. We danced then freely the title song from *Hair* and "Good Morning Sunshine," a number which twinkles, shines, and glows. The record jacket says, "join in, flower children," and though none of us were children of any kind — rather we were women emerging from our hidden places with newly discovered power through dance — we did indeed twinkle, shine, and most definitely, glow.

IMPROVISATIONAL ROCK DANCE WORKSHOP IV

The Rock Workshops evolved through the years and changed as I found new ways to assist women in confronting slippery self-confidence. Workshop IV is the one I use now. Though the lessons differ in content from those of past Workshops, the basic concepts remain the same throughout. Lessons 1 and 2 are concerned with "quality" identification. Next, we study rhythm. In Lesson 4 we work with pure improvisation. No. 5 deals with self-confidence. And Lesson 6 is a shared experience of review and renewal.

LESSON NO. 1

"Expanding" is the underlying theme of Lessons 1 and 2. *Now* is the time to open. Each woman will do so in her own way, at her own speed. I help peel back the petals one by one to expose the sensitive creative dancer at the center. The unfolding happens gradually. Some women use arms for the first time; others stretch their chests. All open to a degree.

Warmup

We jog to the opening cut of *Four*, an album by Tim Wiseberg, the excellent jazz-rock flutist. I find it desirable to lead the stretch dance, to bring the women through a flowing routine that stretches the body completely. (The routine is discussed in Workshop I Lesson 1. Surprisingly, for the most part this has remained the same.) Only in Lessons 5 and 6, after having practiced pure improvisation in No. 4, do I offer the students a more difficult stretch experience. The record used here is the slow, force-

ful "Easy Street" by Edgar Winter. For the isolated dancing, we continue with Tim Wiseberg.

Lesson

As many rock-dancing people do not include "soul"
in their dances nor stray in their floor stomping from the
music's steady, simple beat — indeed, they do not even
perceive musical changes, let alone incorporate them into
their movements — I begin the Workshop with the impera-
tive to listen well and identify qualities. For this exercise I
use Side 1 of *Fire Up* by Merl Saunders, featuring Jerry
Garcia and Tom Fogerty. The four cuts are perfect for my
old stand-by quality labels: *bounce, swing, sway, circles.*
We explore *bounce* and *swing* first. In Lesson 2 we continue with *sway* and *circles.*
I explain that qualities guide the body's performance,
if one but learns through careful listening to assimilate the
subtleties of the music. I assign the qualities to the four
pieces and we listen to a bit of each. I ask the women to
visualize their bodies moving in the fashion of the assigned
quality. Then we begin the record anew and go to work.
I work more slowly and thoroughly now with quality
than I did in past Workshops. I do this because the four
sample qualities are not only guides for "mood" practice
but they represent valuable basic body movements as well.
We must recognize the physical value inherent in practicing
changing qualities. So, we drill extensively in the two qualities of *bounce* and *swing*. (Please refer to Workshop II
Lesson 1 for details on bringing *bounce* and *swing* to the
body.) Being able to use one's natural bounce, swing, or
sway in a dance is important in rock improvisation. As we
practice expressing the emotional states of our dances so
are we learning physical skills that will serve us when we
dance other moods or qualities. For instance, to dance

"funky" requires one to be bouncy. To dance "mellow" may mean combining swing and sway. With more experience each woman will create a dance of depth where all these skills and more are used to form a complex dance of physical and emotional variety. Her dance will have soul. The more one dances, the more expansive her dance becomes.

Free Dance

For the short time remaining we relax with Tim Wiseberg, opening our minds and bodies. I respect the privacy the women require to do this and turn away, relishing the sounds in a dance of my own.

LESSON NO. 2

Warmup

We jog to Chuck Mangione's beautiful flugelhorn and stretch to Jeff Beck's piece " 'Cause We've Just Ended as Lovers." Then back to Mangione for an energetic isolated dancing.

Lesson

In this lesson we practice the qualities of *sway* and *circles*. (Again, the details are in Workshop II Lesson 1.) The record once more is *Fire Up* by Merle Saunders. I remind the women to expand, particularly while dancing the *circles* quality where they may open in space with large arm movements. During this practice people breathe easier, inhaling long draughts of energy and discarding old habits of fear. We work slowly, and when we have mastered these two mood and movement traits we review the entire record, dancing the four qualities of *bounce, swing, sway,* and *circles.*

Finally, I play two Latin-jazz instrumentals by different artists. The only similarity between the pieces is its general category. The mood of one is extremely different than that of the other, an enticement for the perceptive dancer. I play Curtis Mayfield, the quality of which is smooth, then Santana, which is slightly frantic. "First listen only," I suggest as usual. "See yourself moving in your mind's eye. Be aware of where the music centers itself within you and dance from that body part with the appropriate quality."

Free Dance

Often there is no time for free dance in this lesson, but when there is I supply veils from the Isadora days and to a slow piece by Chuck Mangione we explore improvisationally the quality of flugelhorn, veil, and jazz combined.

LESSON NO. 3

Warmup

The Path is used for this lesson's jog, stretch, and isolated dancing. This wonderful album traces jazz from Africa to the American pop disco scene and back to Africa.

Lesson

This lesson deals with aspects of the rock-music beat. First we identify the beat and become familiar with it. I draw from past Workshops to explain the simplicity of the basic rhythm and to transfer the four-count beat to our feet. Sometimes we practice the two-beat stomp as described in Workshop I Lesson 4. Depending upon the needs of each class we may practice a two-gesture pattern as another way of knowing the beat. This is discussed in Workshop II Lesson 5. Most times I introduce the "stop gimmick" of Workshop III Lesson 2. In our busy daily lives we snowball activities, rolling ourselves to somewhere lost within the middle. Stopping action, breathing, and re-energizing ourselves are important functions for us to do. On a crowded dance floor the rhythm, too, runs away with us until our unique dance is buried in the beat. To create a sharp stillpoint before continuing renews one's dance.

A new "beat" exercise I do consists of each woman making small patterns of movement that she repeats throughout a dance. She may do several patterns in one dance or she may do only two or three. She is encouraged to discover these patterns during the isolated dancing. "Pay attention to the movements that emerge automatically from your body's improvisation," I say. "For instance, you may find your hips responding to the beat by making half circles, then full ones. Pick that up; repeat it; make it a discipline-in-rhythm exercise." We continue this practice initiated in the isolated dancing in the lesson when I play "Love to Love you Baby" by Donna Summer. The monotonous beat of this eighteen-minute song is ideal for developing little patterns of dance movement with our arms, hips, feet, or legs. Releasing herself via her patterns to the hypnotic quality of the music allows a dancer to experience thoroughly an absorption into rock rhythm.

Free Dance

I play Donna Summer's song again. The women practice the further surrender of their bodies to its hypnotic trait. Concentration is intense and many dancers enter that difficult "in" stage of movement improvisation whereby new dance patterns evolve automatically for each of them.

LESSON NO. 4

It is apparent to me now that through the years I have considered the last half of each Improvisational Rock Workshop to be Level 2, though never have I used this label. Undoubtedly, a broader dance consciousness sets the tone for the last three lessons of each Workshop. Gradually, we add a spiritual dimension to the purely physical exercises. We come from technical to ethereal considerations and from self's dance to that of another. I do not explain this shift to students. It takes place subtly by way of our activities. What I do say is that in the second half of the Workshop we will study improvisation in depth. We will dance with a greater awareness of others and observe how our doing so affects self-confidence.

Warmup

For the jog and isolated dancing I play the music of jazzist, Tim Wiseberg. Recently, I use mostly rock-jazz, for it offers the dancer many delicate nuances. Jazz, with its tradition of improvisation, well suits my purposes, especially in this lesson in which we study pure movement improvisation. For the stretch dance, "Easy Street" by Edgar Winter.

Lesson

We discuss movement improvisation and read related sections from *Modern Dance* by Cheney and Strader. I explain what being "in" means and how we can attain that state. (Reviewed earlier in the book.) Movement improvisation is new to most women in my classes. They wonder how it can help them dance better. They ask, will they lose control of their dance, relinquish power, become too absorbed? Bad enough in class, but will they make fools of themselves on a public dance floor? So, as always, we begin our practice of improvisation slowly, with the assurance that I will be guiding them and that the classroom is a safe place in which to experiment.

The "helpers" I use are shaker instruments and veils. The brisk Brazilian beat of *Primal Roots* is excellent accompaniment for improvisation with shakers. The women must look at their instruments during their dances. This facilitates concentration and helps eliminate self-consciousness. The focus of each dance is the instrument; the student must work around that focal point. When she concentrates fully, the principle factors of improvisation occur: *movement flows without preplan, and body and mind move as one.*

After dancing two pieces from *Primal Roots* I pass out veils, play *The Tim Wiseberg Band* record, and direct students to the flow of the flute. Now there are two items for concentration, the veils and the flute sounds. We slip into the joyful feeling of improvised flowing. Of course it takes much practice to be "in" every time. For this reason I encourage the women to dance at home between classes.

Free Dance

More of Tim Wiseberg, with veils and then without,

letting the focus become only the flute which so beseeches us to dance.

LESSON NO. 5

Up until now the women have been peeking at each other dancing, while keeping experimentation as private as possible and withdrawing their eyes if they dance by another too closely. In this lesson we confront one another and find it a joyful relief.

Warmup

We jog as usual and do routine isolated dancing. The stretch dance, however, is different. Having worked intensely with improvisation the week before, now we improvise our stretch dances. I play "Cristo Retentor" by Donald Byrd. Slow and haunting, the piece inspires expression of emotion. The women focus on changing levels, letting a slow, strong stretch begin at a high level, evolve to the middle level and, finally, to the floor. Still as deliberate and smooth as possible, the stretch must be brought up again through the levels, ending in a high position. This combination of powerful music and strong movement is a physical and emotional challenge. It offers an opportunity to release rather than retain energy. Lastly, it is an excellent structured exercise in improvisation.

Lesson

I play John Lennon's slow, sad "Isolation" from the *John Lennon/Plastic Ono Band* album. The women are asked to walk about the room in and out one another.

They must be aware of others moving near them, but they are *not* to have eye contact. Easy enough. The second time I play the piece they continue their walks as before, but when they feel the proximity of another, they must stop face-to-face, look directly into the other's eyes, then move on. Throughout the song they confront each other and communicate silently in this fashion. It is important that they do not talk. Nearly everyone does at first. Words furnish a facade behind which the woman crouches for protection. But this is a place of safety. Here she may reveal her vulnerable self to another without needing to giggle, wisecrack, or even smile. She simply may look and be looked upon. The experience aids growth in communication, assertion, and self-confidence.

The next step is to pair with another for an improvisational hand dance. This activity is similar to the mirror exercise described in the "With Others" section of *Creative Dance for Women*, the next segment of this book. The basic purpose of the exercise is to foster a mutual exchange of energy in a flowing, confident manner. The result is a communication in movement between two or more people that creates an additional entity, their dance.

I play a slow rhythmic piece from *Primal Roots*. Standing opposite one another they focus on two items only: the music and the other's hands, from which they may not look away. Attending, they must feel the other's quality of movement and degree of energy. They must surrender to the flow that results. They should not lead aggressively with abrupt, planned movements. At a particular point they will discover they cannot determine who is leading. Sometimes the dance extends automatically to the arms and torso.

For the next dance I play a faster cut from *Primal Roots* and each woman dances alone. However, as she dances she must look at the others with more awareness of them than she has had in past lessons. "Move in and out of each other's dances," I instruct. They must make brief contact. Sometimes a glance is enough. At other times women share rhythms for a few moments.

In the last part of this exercise half the women watch while the others dance. The dancers are encouraged to return the looking. All are reminded this is *not* a judgement time. It is simply a looking and enjoying time. In a while the groups trade activities.

Free Dance

If a woman has done all the interacting she can manage to do for the first time, she is free to dance alone. But I see some students watch for the opportunity to continue contact. This is nice.

LESSON NO. 6

Traditionally, the last lesson of every Improvisational Rock Dance Workshop is a review, though the form differs each time. As I have stated, the evolution of the Workshops, as well as that of my personal growth through dance, has proceeded through years of changes. Finally I have refined the essence of the Rock Workshops to include those elements most conducive to satisfying dance. In this last lesson we emphasize those elements.

Warmup

We jog as usual. The stretch we do is the same as that of No. 5, the preceding lesson. For the isolated dancing, Tim Wiseberg's jazz flute guides us again in the expression of our innovative dances.

Lesson

The quintessence of the Rock Workshops always has been that each woman shall enlarge upon her own style. The Workshops merely provide the tools with which she may accomplish this task. In this lesson we move with free spirit to a series of pieces I play for the implementation of each "tool." In the first dance I remind the women to listen well and begin slowly. Upon becoming centered in her own dance, one must tune in to the environment — to space, others, emotions, objects in the room, contrasts in her movements, limited and expanded dance.

We devote time to "qualities," particularly those of *flow* and *bounce* (smooth and sharp). We give attention to rhythms, varying them, pausing, dancing against a fast basic beat at a deliberate half-time pace. In another dance we rest our favorite body part and work the one through which we have difficulty expressing ourselves.

Finally, we do a movement exercise to challenge the most important trait one must possess in rock dancing, that of self-confidence. Does each woman now believe in the effectiveness of her dance? Is she satisfied with her abilities and pleased with the outcome of her efforts? I play "The Ballad of Danny Bailey," "Dirty Little Girl," and "All the Girls Love Alice," three successive songs from Elton John's *Yellow Brick Road* album. Half the class enjoys dancing while the other half enjoys watching *without judgement*. (I dance *and* I watch, also without judgement.) The first group dances one and a half pieces. At my signal (which is a full-body gesture, for I, too, am ensconced in the dance), one group "waltzes" in, the other out, with the music never stopping. These women have their one and a half songs then. And during the last loud bars I wave back the original group and we dance altogether with high energy to the Workshop's glorious finale.

A FINAL THOUGHT REGARDING THE IMPROVISA-TIONAL ROCK DANCE WORKSHOPS

From the beginning, the second half of each Improvisational Rock Dance Workshop has dealt with attaining abilities that serve one beyond dancing. Always my hope has been that women of the Workshops will use the skills developed in performing successful dance to enlarge and enhance other facets of their lives. The practice of improvisation is an endeavor every woman will find worthwhile in daily life where, with its stresses, we must be confidently flexible and creative to survive.

To improvise is to flow, but it is also to assert. To improvise is *not* to be passive. Rather, it is to tune in, imperceptibly so sometimes, to the energy around us, and affect change with a like degree of influence. Every person needs to feel effective in her culture, and small accomplishments by common citizens are as important to the society and the individual as are major decisions by famous persons. Successful improvisation is a device for implementing a woman's personal power, that trait which has been bruised, battered, and hidden for so long she does not remember it exists.

Moving with an awareness of others, as we do in the second half of the Workshops, is related to communicating and sharing in a greater way than dancing. To sense another's mood and move with it, perhaps contributing feelings of one's own to the act, is indeed a sensitive and sophisticated way to understand the other better, as well as one's self. Respect and compassion follow this exchange between people. To know one is often to love one. Because the word "love" is used so lightly lately, let us say rather that knowledge is wisdom. To be wise in the ways of one another in our world is to contribute to the well being of us all. Self-confidence contributes to the positive interaction between individuals, which is the beginning of knowing each other.

When I speak of self-confidence in dancing I espouse a simple principle: *if your dance feels right it is right*. I tell my students repeatedly that the dance each chooses to do is the correct one. The dances they do in Lesson 6 often are not very much different than those which they did in Lesson 1. In Lesson 6 they do them with more confidence. The cliche, "It's not what you *do* but how you *feel* about it", does have truth.

I feel like the Wizard of Oz bestowing upon myself and my students not a heart, a brain, or courage, but good self-esteem. "But you always had it and didn't know it," I would say. "Where I come from there are people who have personal power, who are creative and effective. We call them successes. But they don't have anything more than you except one thing — self-confidence. And really you've had *that* all along. You just didn't exercise it."

In class we exercise self-confidence in many ways, mainly by allowing ourselves to be watched dancing. As exercise becomes habit each woman will carry an improved self-esteem onto the public dance floor and into the rest of her life.

Stretching and dancing isolated body parts are basic to every Workshop class.

Photos: Meaveen O'Connor

Careful listening allows the music to come to us *before* moving.

When we concentrate we become the music.

"Bounce" "Swing" "Sway" "Circles": Four basic qualities that ready us for Rock.

"Bounce"

"Swing"

"Sway"

"Circles"

Using the physical tools of dance we change levels and shapes to vary mood and design.

We release the body rather than restrict it.

In improvising we reach the state of "in"; then enter the flow.

With extended arms we enlarge our space in dance and in the world.

We do *individual* and *group* improvisations, both *structured* and *free*.

Circles create a holistic network.

"We shake that lovely, loose fat, giving ourselves permission to let it dance, peeking over our shoulders to validate and glorify that beautiful part of our anatomy that we as proper ladies have had to pretend does not exist."

CREATIVE DANCE WORKSHOPS

The Creative Dance Workshop originally was named *Movement Improvisation*. In 1977, after two years of having explored improvisation in Rock dancing, I was anxious to expand the possibilities for movement to other areas of dance. Along with jazz and rock music in the new Workshops we would experiment with varieties of other sounds, as well as with feelings, physical properties, and group dancing. Also, we would familiarize ourselves with the primary elements of dance movement — space, force, rhythm, and locomotor and non-locomotor moves.

The Movement Improvisation Workshop was six weeks long. It was offered as a non-technique class for women of all abilities where they could give themselves permission to explore individual and group improvisation in a safe atmosphere. The first classes were small. After making inquiries I discovered the title was intimidating. Women wondered what threatening activity they should expect from a course called "movement improvisation." So, I changed the name to *Creative Dance for Women*, a gentler title. At the onset of each new Workshop I made a point of discussing with the students their thoughts on creative dance, what I considered creative dance to be, and what we would be doing in class. This seemed to relax us all. The course has been called *Creative Dance* ever since.

The format of every class is the same. The first half hour is a structured period, a routine warmup time. In these classes I am less interested in warming our bodies, however, than I am in warming our souls. I am most anxious to tempt, tickle, and entice forth in each person her desire to dance joyfully. For, as in all kinds of improvisational movement, a special characteristic of creative dance is its function as a tool for activating self-confidence and raising self-esteem. With the creation of a dance a woman experiences her power to move in a resourceful way, a prerequisite for making positive personal choices.

Gradually we warmup that shy, wild desire to dance. We cajole and coddle it, cherishing nervous giggles, wiggling hips, spontaneous grins. During every beginning we loosen our bodies by shaking tightness away. I mention Raggedy Ann and share with the students my vision of no bones, no muscles, and therefore, no tension, as together we shake arms, hands, shoulders without knots, heads that bob on flexible necks. (If I must use the image of a doll, at least I avoid Barbie with the slickness and inflexibility of her tiny perfect plastic body.) For the shaking exercise I use African drums or Brazilian music.

We jog, do a stretch dance, and perform improvisational isolated dancing. The warmup activities are similar to those of the Rock Workshops, with the emphasis here particularly upon letting go of inhibitions. Also, the music used is similar to that of the Rock Workshops. The following list consists of music types used in the warmup period: folk and ethnic, especially Russian, African, Brazilian, and Middle Eastern; rock; jazz; blues; music I call "spacey" rock or "experimental ethereal," like that of Pink Floyd and Mike Oldfield, where electrified and electronic instruments are used in innovative ways.*

* For complete list of music for each section see Music Index for Creative Dance Workshop.

After the warmup we move on to the "problem" or "challenge." Because the range of material from which one may choose is vast, every Creative Dance Workshop is different. What I have endeavored to do for the purposes of this book, therefore, is to group lessons into six major categories, each of which represents a compilation of related movement activities that may serve as suggestions for teachers and individual women dancers in developing their own creative dancing ideas.

I IMPROVISATION

Improvisation is the background against which creative dance becomes defined. It is the basis upon which I build every class I teach. To have a satisfying creative dance experience one must feel free to improvise. In class I explain the concept of "flow" which underlies improvisation in movement, using the words "flow" and "improvise" interchangeably. (For discussion of "flow" see The Psychology of Flow, Page 33, Part I.) Upon explaining "flow," I emphasize one need not perform only sustained or smooth movements. Rather, "flow" denotes concentration that carries any type gesture along a continuum of dance movement. After one has learned to improvise alone, she may use that skill in dancing with others.

In all lessons I furnish structure for guidance through this new experience of improvisation, an experience which often leaves one feeling revealed and vulnerable. Occasionally I open a Workshop with the following improvisation: We make a circle. I volunteer to be first. "My name is Beverly and I really love to dance." As each woman says the last part, she performs a movement. Before starting I had suggested and demonstrated some simple gestures. They might jump in a circle, wiggle hips, or make a pattern with arms. The next woman in the circle says her name and does her movement. Then she repeats the refrain, ". . . and I really love to dance," and performs the prior movements as well. The last person says the refrain several times, dancing all the previous movements. The ice is broken. Everyone has moved. What is more, they have heard and said "I really love to dance" so many times that they have created an urgent impetus, indeed, to prove the statement.

One of the basic dance improvisation "problems" I consider essential to present in classes is a thorough flowing experience. This exercise *does* happen to be slow, smooth, and sustained. I use "Cristo Retentor" from the record, *A New Perspective*. The music is soulful, with a chanting chorus that strains one's emotions and a trumpet whose wails arouse and caress. To begin, the women sit on the floor. (The students wear any comfortable clothing, with feet bare.) First, we listen only, hearing the instruments, letting the music in, breathing with it, and feeling its pulse. The piece lasts five minutes. The second time we move head and hands. Still sitting, we watch our hands, letting them follow a natural course of movement. Nothing is planned. Nothing is rushed. The third time the women's whole bodies respond. (Complete familiarity with the music by then eases anxieties.) They may continue sitting or they may stretch out in full-body contact with the floor. Some alternate between lying and sitting. The fourth time we do a full-body dance from sitting to standing and back down again in a steady flow. This is not a choreographed dance. They must let the flowing occur without anticipating or caring where it will take them. Sometimes we repeat the fourth part.

Often the following week's class builds on this exercise. We improvise with another; we flow together. This second activity is not recommended for every beginning creative dance group. If the group is cohesive, if it is willing to risk and open easily, we experiment. Otherwise the problem is too advanced. The series of exercises progresses as follows: First, each woman focuses on one part of her own body, hands for instance. She watches them as she dances them only, with no music. She must concentrate on their flow. Secondly, each woman takes a partner and mirrors the *one* part of her partner's body that is dancing. They take turns being the mirror. No sound. Third, this time when concentrating on each other they *do not mirror but complement* the other's movement in any way that flows. They may use the same body part or another, the same movement or a different one. Still there is no music. They take turns beginning. Fourth, we do the same with music. I often play the slow piece, " 'Cause We've Ended as Lovers," by Edgar Winter. Fifth, we dance as a group to the same music. We do not focus on one person but feel the magnetism of group movement and yield to its power. No one person is an overt leader. Noone prescribes the movements. They evolve smoothly, and new dance emerges without force which would break the flow.

As the women become practiced in allowing themselves to flow, they open their bodies more. As the need to protect themselves against criticism diminishes, gestures broaden and bodies fill more space. With this opening comes increased flexibility, both physical and mental. I find two activities particularly good in aiding the opening process. In the more structured of the two I play "Chime Blues" by the New Orleans Preservation Hall Band on the record, *Sweet Emma*. We take turns dancing across the floor, *leading with a different part of our bodies every time*. Each student creates a dance of her own style, making it as long or short as she wishes and letting the designated body part carry her across the room. Legs, arms, hips are easy to lead with. The harder parts are the neglected ones: upper back, the neck, the underarm. We let ourselves laugh and yelp as we slither New Orleans style to the low-down beat which is a reminder to us that dancing is a process of letting go.

The second activity for opening the body is a free dance to "The Tenth World" from Joni Mitchell's album, *Don Juan's Reckless Daughter*. It is a long piece, featuring conga and bongo drums with repetitious rhythm. Music of this type with its hypnotic quality guarantees the means for the steadily evolving movements that comprise an improvisational flow. Before beginning we talk about opening places in our bodies that have been deprived of music's touch. The women are to give themselves to the drums as they would to a lover, feeling, seeing, and hearing nothing else. In my own dancing to this record I have discovered myself opening the underarm area, from the upper arm to the outer breast, a hidden spot we keep locked tight.

At a time near the end of a Workshop when the students have begun to own a feeling for improvisation, we devote a session to group movement with a parachute. (In some Workshops, however, if the ambiance seems adventurous, I present the parachute "cold turkey" the first class and then use it again in the last class so we may compare sessions and measure progress.) For this activity, I use continuous music that flows in improvisational fashion from one mood to the next. Mike Oldfield's music is ideal. Side 1 of *Hergest Ridge* is one of my favorites.

Before beginning we have discussion in preparation for the challenge. I remind the women to be sensitive to the music's changes and to others' movements. They should be aware of the group mood and focus on it. They must keep the dance in their bodies, not in their heads, for if they lead or choreograph the movements they will have stepped outside the flow. We begin by each holding a spot at parachute's edge. The entire group sits or stands. I never direct them to do one or the other. Instead, I follow with curiosity. Unspoken group decision, differing with each class, governs the starting. To me this is interesting because it is indicative of the power of non-vocal group improvisation and the willingness of people to partake of it.

The women are cautioned against having expectations and we begin slowly, perhaps fluttering the parachute with small hand movements. This can lead to arm waving, then to full body rise and fall. And the improvisation is on its way, from quiet music to loud, from wild to gentle dance. Sometimes it happens, through a delicate evolution of the dance and with non-verbal consent and participation of all, that one woman will capture the parachute. She may roll herself up in it; she might run the room's length, trailing it behind her. The rest complement her act with appropriate movements, returning to contact with the parachute as it feels correct to do so. Often when concentration and focus is strong the parachute seems life-like, dancing of its own volition and leading us deeper into improvisation. When the dance ends we feel we have shared something special. We are enriched.

People who dance extensively know that movement can be meditation. I combine movement meditation and movement improvisation in an exercise we perform lying on our backs on the floor. I play the record *Music for Zen Meditation and Other Joys* which features clarinet, koto, and shakuhachi (bamboo flute.) The women close their eyes and lie still. I dim the lights if possible. First, they must take time to allow the quiet sounds to settle into their bodies. The impetus for movement must come only when body and sounds are integrated. Movement proceeds extremely slowly. When the flute's song fills one's head and a hand feels it has become the clarinet's sweet note lifted from the floor, then only does each woman perform movement meditation. She moves at the sound's speed. She moves only slightly, mostly with hands at first. With her hands she may travel the space above her or the warm wooden floor beneath her. She may explore her body, a leg or stomach, in a quiet, gentle way. The only requirement is that she progress slowly and smoothly. It is better that she move only a finger but *be with the sound*, than move her whole body, only to rush past it. Body and sound must function as one. At the height of meditation the mind is clear of all thought while the body moves automatically.

Beginners sometimes relax totally but do not get to the next step, that of starting the movement. It is better to make that mistake, however, than to force movement. For if one forces she has not even begun the process. In time and with practice, movement meditation can be performed with a variety of music types and body gestures. Some women do this meditation on a regular basis alone at home. It is a fine way to begin one's day or to end it. Also, it provides the perfect ending for a class session.

II   THE PHYSICAL TOOLS

Archeology deals with the basics of Anthropology, the "stones and bones" of it. The basics of dance are the "steps and shapes." These are our physical tools. As the ability to improvise ignites one's desire to create dances, so may knowledge of locomotor and non-locomotor dance movements provide means for actually doing so. So, in class we review the eight basic steps of dance — skip, gallop, jump, leap, run, slide, hop, walk. We also devote sessions to the non-locomotor actions of our bodies in dance — shaking, stretching, changing levels, creating line and space designs, to name a few.

Regarding the steps, we are playful. We skip, gallop, and jump, as children do. We experiment with variations, like a skip turn or a high gallop. For music I use European folk songs and a four-beat rhythmic exercise record. After practicing the steps we create our own folk dances. For this I divide the class into four sections. On a given night there may be three or four in each group. They are instructed to choose three steps (or more), work them into a simple pattern, and continue to repeat the pattern. I suggest they move in various directions — in circles or lines, backward or forward, together or apart. The dances may be as simple or as complex as the members wish. A sample dance is created as follows: The members make a circle, *slide* four steps left, then four right. Drop hands, *skip* backwards four, *jump* four times, *skip* forward four. And begin again. Voila, a folk dance! Hand, arm, and upper body movements may be included. The number of possible combinations is endless. Each group practices in a corner before presenting its dance to the others.

Then two groups combine and teach each other their dances, for a longer, six-step dance, repeated. Now we have two instead of four dances. In turn, the two groups may teach each other, for a grand dance. Whether or not the class reaches the last stage, the project of making a dance, increasing its complexity, and performing it with high energy is exciting. Someone always says, "That was fun!" This is an important clue for teachers. For the entire teaching/dancing/learning process is a failure if we do not bring joy to class. Without joy our dances lose their value as catalysts for opening ourselves: to each other, to the world, and ultimately to our sense of latent personal power.

Regarding the non-locomotor movements, we familiarize ourselves with the changing contours of our dancing bodies. We practice making shapes — bent, twisted, straight, open, closed. We bring those changing shapes through different levels in space — high, medium, and low. We make dances with rounded or angular shapes, first alone, then with a partner. We experiment with opposites. We create soft dances, then hard ones, light and heavy, bent and straight, high and low, fast and slow.

For structuring lessons in the Creative Dance classes I use mostly the guided exploration method. We are introduced to the problem — *strong shapes*, for instance. We

play with it, work on it, experiment. Then we create improvised dances of strong shapes to varied music.

However at times I stray from exploration, development, and practice. Occasionally I offer a highly structured
lesson, like the following exercise for non-locomotor body
qualities. Using *stretch, bend, twist,* and *shake,* we dance
to "Walking' Blues" by the Butterfield Blues Band. To
four beats the women *stretch* in one direction. To the next
four they *stretch* out in another direction, perhaps at a different level. (There is much opportunity for improvising
within each prescribed movement.) During the next eight
beats they make four different *bent body shapes,* two
counts each. (Many women are out of touch with the flex-
ing possibilities of their bodies, either from physical disuse
or emotional fear.) For the next eight slow beats they
twist themselves, starting with arms perhaps, moving into
the torso, maybe the legs. (Blues music demands deliberate,
thorough movements.) In the last eight beats they *shake* a
part of their bodies or all of it. (Shaking is a wonderful
loosening device, and its variations are many.) As this last
eight counts end, the dance pattern is begun again. *Stretch,
stretch, shape, shape, shape, shape, t-w-i-s-t, shake.* And repeated. Soon one movement flows into the next in a
honey-smooth blues mood. Using music of the emotions,
like blues, is an effective way to release our inner dancer.

One may create variations of this exercise by substitu-
ting other non-locomotor movements — *push, swing,
dodge,* for example. Another variation of this theme is
made possible by combining non-locomotor moves with
locomotor ones. For instance, giving four beats to each, alternate a blues walk with a strong stretch. The possibilities
are endless. A teacher may make the exercise as simple or
as complex as she feels suits the class. Using the original
pattern, I often suggest eight beats of locomotion in place
of the twist part. This lets our dance travel (as our lives,
too, may move to other places.) Again, the right music is

the key for success in this study. Blues or New Orleans jazz kindles the soul which fires the body.

There are a number of other short, simple studies I incorporate in Creative Dance sessions to bring students in touch with body qualities and spacial perceptions. Briefly, here are fragments of those activities with which the reader may experiment and upon which she may build. 1) We walk, run, or skip; then turn, jump, and freeze in a shape, either angular or bent, at a high, medium, or low level. 2) We work on a series of shapes, opening our bodies, stretching them to the utmost, closing or twisting. Often I play hand instruments for accompaniment — different type drums, a tambourine, or shakers. (I let their movements lead my playing, rather than vice versa.) 3) In another series, we come to each other, touching, freezing, creating a group sculpture. Sometimes we move over, under, and between one another for a feeling of changing in space. 4) We dance alternately low, then high, melting to the floor and growing into space. 5) We stop suddenly, holding a shape and noting it, increasing our body awareness, then continuing from that frozen shape to flow.

Practice of these and other basic movement exercises not only teaches the women the fundamentals of dance, it facilitates their beginning efforts to create dances with others as well.

III WITH OTHERS

A few pages back I spoke of using a parachute in group improvisation. This is an exciting but difficult way to dance with other people. Mostly I prefer to progress gradually to the degree of freedom in movement necessary to meet this challenge. For this purpose I rely on a standard "with others" series, which I present at a prior class. This series is a long one, a ten-step unit, but it is comprehensive and well worth the effort to do it. For it takes the dancer from deliberate non-contact with others to total group improvisation. I have borrowed steps from this series to use in the Improvisational Rock Dance Workshops. I refer the reader to Rock Workshop IV Lesson 5 for further insights into the related process of women coming together in both rock and creative dance.

Again I use the slow, plaintive song, "Isolation," from the *John Lennon/Plastic Ono Band* record.

Step 1: The women must walk around the room in isolation. They are aware of the other people about them but noone may have contact, even with eyes. Purposely, they avoid one another.

Step 2: The second time I play the song, they walk again. This time each person must come directly to another, pause before her, look into her eyes, then move on. There may be no verbal connection. Each woman will have encountered the others several times when the music ends.

Step 3: The women pair up now for a mirror exercise. There is no music. Half lead until I stop them and direct the second half to lead. With this preplanned arrangement there is no doubt who is leading, who is following.

Step 4: Still no music. Now they take the lead from each other without stopping movement and without having verbal agreement. Leadership is exchanged between bodies automatically until one is not sure whether she leads or follows. An energy flow has been created between them.

Step 5: The same exchange, *with* the music, "Isolation."

Step 6: I change the music to *Drums of Passion* (African), Side 1, Cut 2. Discarding the mental mirror between them but retaining the same flowing exchange of leading and following, they must now do a hand improvisation dance.

Step 7: Still in partners they perform an *angular* dance

together, complementing one another's gestures. (The study of *angular* or *line* and *bent* or *rounded* shapes is mentioned in *II The Physical Tools*. The women will have practiced shapes prior to this series.) Then they do a *rounded* shape dance together.

Step 8: They must let go the security of familiar partners. They choose new ones and repeat the *angular* and *rounded* shape dances. Still noone leads; noone follows.

Step 9: Continuing with African music, they do individual dances again in an *adjacent* space to each other. This space arrangement serves as transition from partner to group dance. In dancing adjacent spaces each woman must stay out of the physical space of the others. But in order not to lose the contact they have created and which they will need to do a group dance, I instruct them to look at each other, to be connected mentally or emotionally. They stay only in adjacent space for now to further foster an acute recognition of what it means to dance separate and how it feels to dance together. In a little while they leave neighboring spaces and dance exclusively in *connecting* spaces. That is, each woman *must* stay in another's physical space (that area being as far as one can reach.) The women must take responsibility for noone's being excluded from the invisible net connecting them all. Someone always is no more than an arm's length away, and they certainly may touch each other. A community of dancing exists. A group feeling has been established. (Teachers may find it convenient to borrow Step 9, *adjacent and connecting spaces*, for a lesson alone.)

Step 10: Now they do the group improvisation, the ultimate "with others" dance activity. I play Paul Horn's *Inside*, chants and flute inside the Taj Mahal. The women begin in a connecting space formation, which means they are close together. The echoing sounds guide them into flowing, interconnected movement. Remembering the mirror exercises just performed, they surrender the inclination to dominate by leading with overt gestures. Instead, with sustained concentration and delicate perception, what often results in addition to a successful group dance is a satisfying group movement meditation.

The ten-step "with others" series is valuable for providing experience and promoting confidence with which we may proceed to other group movement activities.

In dance, the opposite of isolation is integration. And nothing is more integrated than a circle. Circle dancing has an historical and traditional background and many possibilities for use in a Creative Dance class. The circle symbol is powerful, for it means eternity. Its cyclic form denotes rebirth and renewal. In a dance circle the women are linked together, each one coming from another and continuing to the next. When a circle is formed by the connecting of hands a current of energy inspires and supports our awakening to dance.

My circle dance activity is so simple and yet so satisfying that I am convinced its success lies literally in the hands of the women. Our interconnection makes us feel good and, thus, function well. For one dance I use Ravi Shankar's record, *The Sounds of India*. We dance an entire side, about twenty minutes. I say simply, "follow me," and I never do the same dance twice. Mostly the movements I do are gentle and small. I have more interest in tuning us in to the music and each other than in creating an extravaganza. I prefer to lead the entire dance rather than break the mood by speaking to ask others to lead. As in the mirror exercises, often what happens is a feeling of flowing begins and the conscious effort to lead and follow softens, nearly dispersing completely. Sometimes another woman assumes the lead, as they have been advised beforehand they may do if it is not forced.

During the dance we hold hands most of the time. As I said, the movements are slight. We may simply bend knees or lift arms. We may change levels or turn slowly. And we keep coming back to holding hands, giving and taking energy, beginning anew.

In other classes we have performed the same dance with Middle Eastern music which is used for belly dancing. Though the rhythm of this music is not as hypnotic as that of the Indian music, the dance we do is sensual, reflecting that characteristic of the American woman so in need of honest expression. Other times I use European folk music, though the beat is more harsh and masculine. This music invites interruption so we may retreat and rest. (However, we slow down only, rather than stop. For once begun, we must obey our personal imperatives to continue dancing.) At these rest pauses we change leaders, each woman taking a turn to infuse something of herself to the magical circuit of movement.

For another circle dance I use Brazilian music from Sergio Mendes' *Primal Roots*. We use Side 1, cuts 1, 2, 3, and 5, with stopping in between. During the first cut we do ordinary circle dancing which I lead. In the second cut we move in conga line fashion, allowing a woman to remain leader as long as she wishes to do so. She dances to the end of the line when she is ready to relinquish her contribution as the dominating creative energy. I caution the women to let go the compulsion to duplicate exactly the step of the leader. "Just tune in to her mood, pick up her rhythm and garnish it with your own style." During Cut 3 we re-make a circle, take turns being leader as it suits us each to do so. Through Cut 5 we go from circle to conga line and back to circle, changing formations and leaders with ease.

Another example of a circle dance is one in which we use small hand instruments. The music is *Drums of Passion*, by Olatumji. One woman dances in the center. When she leaves someone takes her place. The pulse of the dance is constant. The women may discard the instruments if they choose to and they may stop when they get tired, as many do. As the group gets smaller, the remaining energy becomes condensed and builds in intensity, as does the music. The dancing becomes super-charged. The flow is frantic. Because there is no time to think, the dance is completely kinesthetic and improvisational. As we end, I am reminded of the tigers around Little Black Sambo whose chase was so interconnected they melted, blending together. We are of a like consistency, our salty sweat and sweet energy mingling, creating one product too, not butter but dance.

Another dance activity we do with others stresses awareness of outer sounds and inner imperatives. Returning to Paul Horn's *Inside*, we make slow, sustained movements with one or more other persons. Mostly hands and arms guide us. The dance is semi-private, semi-public. We flow with another until soulful flute carries us back to ourselves. Floating around the room, in and out of people, is a comfortable way to connect.

For the second part of this exercise, we do movement meditation lying on the floor. (This is described in *I Improvisation*.) The music, *Music for Zen Meditation and Other Joys*. In a while I end the music with one, quiet comment. "Continue moving to no music, rising and joining with others." The meditation momentum carries each person up to connect with the others. One watching witnesses a slow-motion movie without sound. Quite easily the women continue the flow begun with music. When the dance is over, the women feel when to stop. Without being told, they sense the end of the silent cycle.

IV SOUNDS

There are other instances in which dance evolves from silence. In one exercise we use the environmental elements of the class space for dance accompaniment. Having previously worked with the physical tools, the women are asked to create a movement piece from the design of the room. They must notice its lines, light, and mood. I ask questions. Is the room spacious or cramped? Do the ceiling beams render an angular feeling to the room? Is there softness anywhere, or is it bare and hard? Do the floors lend warmth? How will the colors affect the dance? Is it a fast or slow room? Relaxed or frantic? What about its rectangular shape? How will the trees outside the windows change your dance? After some consideration the women design their individual dances based on the room's physical properties and personality. Re-creating a room in a ten-minute silent dance by changing body shapes and varying movement qualities is an exhilarating and unusual experience.

Another activity with no sound involves visualizations. The women sit quietly with eyes closed as I describe a scene. Sometimes it is an ocean scene, sometimes a spring day with singing birds. At the end of the description I suggest that their bodies long to merge with the scene, to become it. "When the time feels right, begin slowly with your eyes closed to dance this scene." They may open eyes soon, provided they maintain the mood. Some dances are a reenactment of the picture in their mind's eye, with objects becoming body shapes. Sometimes dances symbolize feelings about the scene. The dances are as individual as the women are different.

In another case poetry is a sound to which we dance. I use short poems, reading them first for listening. The women may decide whether to represent the message of the poem, the rhythm of the lines, or a combination of both.

One poem, called "Centering",[1] reads as follows: Drawing in and hoarding / like a mother hen / that part of me / which is dispersed / nearly disintegrated / and nurturing it.

---

1.   From *Supermom Wonderwife*, by the author, Morningsun Publications.

In another instance, the women dance without preparation to the poem, "Supermom",2 responding in movement to the rhythm of the words and the tone of my voice.
I'm Mother, like mercury, / everlasting in plasticity, / Ac-
commodating. / Waiting / to be interrupted / from my
waiting. / Ignore me / or pour me / into any niche of need.

Sometimes I give homework. "Turn on the radio and
dance to the first sound you hear, be it music, news, talk
show, commercial, or electronic static!" This assignment
serves to open the students further to a world of constant
movement possibilities.

A most effective "sound" exercise is the one in which I
play small musical instruments, each in turn. The students
respond with bodies matching the tone, mood, intensity,
and rhythm of what they hear. Of course the interpretations differ. A woman may move only a few fingers to the
sound of a tiny bell or shake her whole body to the tambourine. She may travel with strong steps to a drum or
slither full length on the floor to the jangling of a chain.
Often I group sounds that lead the body in a natural pro-
gression from one kind of movement to another. (As in
the following sentence the ear is lead from one sound to
the next.) For an example, staccato sticks evoke sharp
shapes that evolve to bolder ones as the bongo begins.

Moving to the sounds of electronic music offers yet
another dimension into which we may expand. In one instance I use the electronic score of Warner Jepson composed for Carlos Carvajal's production, *Totentanz* or
Dance of Death. This piece is an interpretation of medieval
Spring, the season of feasting and fasting, of death and
new life. The sounds are extreme, from low-tone pulsa-
tions to anxious, high-pitched screeches when Death, mar-
velously caped, lurks on stage, dancing surreptitiously
amongst the others. I ask the women to give themselves

2.   Also from *Supermom Wonderwife*.

completely to the sounds. Because the music is so unusual, it suggests a wide range of moods. People respond to it in many differing ways. Sometimes I tell the story-line first. On other occasions I give the women no information whatsoever, asking them to remain vulnerably open to interpreting exactly what they hear. It takes time to become comfortable with this strange music. Therefore, we dance at least twenty minutes without stopping. The dance is always successful but difficult.

Another time we enact some foolishness as we dance Side 2 of the record, *The Electronic Spirit of Erik Satie*. A commentator titters as he announces for us the titles in French and in English, "Five Grins, or Mona Lisa's Mustache," (four minutes) and "Sports and Amusements" (fourteen minutes), to name two. The avant-garde Erik Satie himself has this to say about these pieces: "It is clear that the Deflated, the Insignificant, the Puffed-up will not appreciate these works. Let them swallow their beards! Let them dance on their own stomachs!"

This music counteracts the too serious approach we take to dance at times. Dancing is joyous. It is release rather than control. It is one of the valuable ways by which we may experience our lives and ourselves. With Erik Satie we cavort and play. Dancing is the happy tool, the monkey wrench we lightly toss occasionally, to stir us up, to make us grin and shake and laugh, and then begin again.

V   INTERPRETATIONS

In addition to electronic music, I include more traditional scores for class interpretation. Three such records include *The Snow Goose* by the rock group, Camel, *Misa Criolla*, the Catholic mass set against rhythms of Argentine folk music, and Chuck Mangione's movie score for *Chil-*

dren of Sanchez.

The Snow Goose is a story by Paul Gallico about friendship between a lonely, outcast old man living on the marsh of the English coast, a young girl, and a beautiful snow goose. The story tells of the man's service and sacrifice at the Battle of Dunkirk in World War I, the flight of the goose instinctively returning to nature after having been friends with humans, and the sweet sadness of the girl left alone. It is a gripping story of love and caring. The group, Camel, has made a record in rock-jazz music of the story.

It starts with quiet music called "The Great Marsh." One feels the atmosphere of a marsh at sunrise. The story continues on both sides of the record with music especially for the old man, the girl, the goose, their friendship, the war, the sinking of the old man's boat, the bird departing, the girl alone, and finally the great marsh again.

The week before I suggest the class read the story, which we discuss. There is an album note for each titled record cut. I read these aloud beforehand so there will be familiarity with the music as one cut leads into the next. Once we begin I do not stop the record but do call out the name of each cut as it begins so we will not get lost in the story. Stopping would hinder the improvisational process.

The women may respond to the story in a variety of ways. They may dance the sounds alone. They may interpret the tale literally. Or, their dances may represent the mood only. Of course they may combine all approaches. Some parts of the record are harder than others to dance. Sometimes the women slip in and out of the flow. I ask that they keep concentrating to persevere through this new movement challenge. By the last cut, "The Great Marsh" repeated, which allows a quiet, gentle end to the dance, we have experienced thoroughly emotion in motion.

I was introduced to the *Misa Criolla* when I saw it performed by six women dancers in the vast Unitarian Church of San Francisco. It moved me totally to see a solemn religious ceremony enacted in dance against the passion of Latin folk music. I recognized its possibilities for the Creative Dance class. As with *The Snow Goose*, advance preparation is necessary. Finding ways to encourage variety of movement is most important. Therefore, for a practice exercise I recite particular words which the women must interpret in dance. I discovered that when I said the words without music there was a tendency for the students to pantomime, to act-out rather than dance. For this reason I cast the words first on a background of Argentine folk music. The second time I recite the words with no music, however, to remind the women it is possible to dance with *no* sound. Here are the words: prayer, gaiety, church, priest, shawl, alter, nun, cross, Christian, holy, fiesta, choir, peasant, folk dance, chalice, mantilla.

In another preparation each woman is given a large white, filmy curtain, her shawl or mantilla, which she may use and discard as she pleases during the *Misa Criolla*. We practice ways to use this prop. We talk of coming together in the dance. We decide we may dance with another and part again. I remind them to change pace with mood, to walk through parts that may be too difficult to dance but not to stop moving altogether. They must change levels and remember to use the floor. Then we indulge in the *Misa Criolla*, experiencing the joyful release of fiesta combined with the somber meditation of a mass.

Anthropologist Oscar Lewis' biography, *Children of Sanchez*, an account of the Mexican people, was made into a movie recently, for which Chuck Mangione wrote and recorded a two-record sound track. "It is not a typical sound track but my personal selection from the twenty-three hours of music I composed for it," says Chuck Mangione in the album notes. Presented in traditional operatic form, this jazz score comprises an overture and a finale, with four record sides of music reflecting the moods of titles such as "Pilgrimage Part 1 and 2," "Market Place," and "Death Scene." "Writing and recording this music was one of the most intense and emotional experiences of my life," Mangione states. "I consider it to be some of the strongest music that has ever come from within me."

In class I use only one cut from the score, the familiar, "Consuelo's Love Theme," a seventeen-minute piece representing feelings in depth of a passionate people. The preparation exercises number three. The music demands sweeping, continuous gestures that cover much space. Arms can carry us long distances when we draw wide designs with them. For the first exercise we dance with arms, reaching, scooping, swirling. For contrast the students must hold arms in abeyance at their sides as they dance. They discover readily the advantages of using arms fully.

Related to this exercise is the second one which deals with "open" and "close." Having worked in previous classes with opening the body to movement, we now dance alternately with opened and closed shapes. "Feel the difference," I say, "and decide how you will use both in 'Consuelo's Love Theme.'"

The third preparation concerns isolated dancing. It is a reminder to devote the body's entire energy supply to one body part at a time, to one movement at a time. For this we take turns moving across the floor leading with one body part. (This is discussed fully in I Improvisation.)

When we are ready for "Consuelo's Love Theme," which is only one cut of many teachers may choose to use from this exciting recording, I remind the women to listen intensely before beginning movement, to allow themselves emotional involvement with the music, to use arms extensively, and to rest if necessary without stopping. Lastly, after remembering all the suggestions, they must forget them and dance devotedly, trusting their bodies to pleasure themselves through space.

VI HOLISTIC DANCE

The term "holistic" is as appropriately assigned to dance as it is to many other endeavors today. "Holism," rooted in the Greek word meaning whole, is a term coined by J. C. Smuts (1870-1950) to designate the tendency in nature to produce wholes (bodies or organisms) from the ordered grouping of unit structures. The Oxford English Dictionary defines "holism" as a general approach to human behavior based on the view that man is a unified organism in whom biological, psychological, and sociocultural aspects are fundamentally integrated. It is an approach in general which emphasizes the study of wholes or totalities.

All my students, from the youngest child to the oldest woman, are instructed constantly to dance with their whole bodies, their whole selves. "Forget your feet," I tell the rock students bent on doing steps while the rest of their bodies suffer suspended animation. "Let the dance emanate from your center self, with your entire body joining in." In the children's classes we give our noses a little dance, and our ears, and even your eyelashes have a dance of their own, not to mention feet, fingers, tummies, and ponytails, until they are dancing all together.

Likewise, in all the women's classes we dance totally to the utmost boundaries of our bodies. The body's dance is born within, emanates out to the skin and, often, beyond. Every body surface is alive as the dancer strives to unite with her surrounding universal space in total communion with the all. In class I use a more earthy approach to this concept. We remain in the physical realm and concentrate on awakening every body part. "Remember you have bottoms too," I may say. "Wiggle them, jiggle them in a whole-body stomp."

In holistic dance the emphasis is placed on the senses and the emotions. We need not fear we are neglecting the intellect, however, for we could not perform any dance without the brain's participation. Indeed, in creative dance we strive continually to turn off the head and let the dance be of the body, of the senses and emotions. The theme of many first classes in the Creative Dance workshops is "get out of your head and into your body."

In classes dealing directly with emotions I have worked with four — fear, anger, sadness, joy. Taking one emotion at a time we enact three problems. First we do a series of body shapes suggestive of the emotion. By so doing we give it physical form. I instruct the women to think "joy" (or whatever emotion we are dancing.) "Ready, *shape*," I keep repeating, and as the shapes continue to evolve, the body is transformed to "joy."

Next, each person improvises a short dance. I accompany them on the drum as they use their changing shapes to create movement. One feels the emotion in the air. Finally, we pair up, creating a dance to my drum accompaniment. Let us say the emotion is "anger." The atmosphere becomes charged and sharp, the shapes exaggerated and strong. We snap about; we plunge forward and back. Sometimes bodies strike into one another, but the purpose of the activity is maintained — *anger is being expelled through movement* and respect for each other is perpetuated throughout. This is difficult, for besides dancing anger, each person also must dance in relation to another's angry body. The other emotions are easier.

Once, a woman, a friend of mine, paired with a person with whom she was upset in their personal lives. She told me later the dance enabled her to express the anger she felt for her partner. Though the pairing process had been casual I do not believe their partnership was coincidental. It was, however, therapeutic and holistic.

Another holistic dance exercise dealing with feelings involves dancing beneath various colored bed linens. The week prior I ask each woman to bring to class a colored sheet. Sometimes people bring silk or rayon ones; texture adds another dimension to the experience. With the sheets draping our bodies we do a series of five-minute dances. Light coming through the linens creates an all blue world for a dancer, or an orange one. The colored music of their private environments frees them to feel and express special, hidden characteristics of themselves. One set of music is as follows: Tschaikovsky's *Pathetique Symphony*, first movement, Christopher Parkening on *Parkening Plays Bach*, Side 1 Cut 2, Rimsky Korsakov's *Schaherazade*, first movement, Erik Satie's *Trois Gymnopedies*. The women move from mood to mood, releasing energy through dance. Sometimes we trade colors, but usually we stay with one sheet only. Occasionally a dancer cannot remain confined beneath the sheet. She prefers using her sheet flamboyantly, waving it, rolling in it, swirling with it. We always take time at the end to discuss the experience.

In another holistic dance we explore three female roles, those of *daughter, lover,* and *mother.* First we practice with veils for a sense of how they may enhance our dances. We whirl and wave them. We wear them walking and roll up in them on the floor. Finally, we spread them out as children do and sit on them.

We are now little girls and ready to dance the first role, that of *daughter.* I use the simple four-beat practice music on the children's record, *Dance-a-long.* Perky and childlike, it sounds like jumprope and playgrounds. The women dance in carefree abandon. They must recall and recapture the spirit of the child within them. They have permission to be light and bouncey, silly and uninhibited. They use their veils to interact with one another, feigning quarrels, chasing each other, or dancing arm-in-arm.

The next role we dance is that of *lover.* I play the Arabian music from the *Nutcracker Ballet.* If they desire they may begin on the floor once again, feeling the warm sensuality of the waxed wood, wrapping or rolling in the veils. If they choose to begin standing, they must melt to the floor at some time during the dance. Each woman is encouraged to dance seductively and to be in touch with her sexuality. Because of its immediacy, this role usually is the easiest to portray.

Even if the women have never been mothers they succumb to the heart-rending music, "Cristo Retentor." I use it for the *mother* role. A friend told me it reminds her of a Kathe Kollwitz painting in which a mother and child are torn apart by death. For some this dance is sad. Women dance to memories of mothers. They dance personal interpretations of motherhood. The dance is slow but not always spiritually burdensome. Motherhood for some means happy dancing.

At the end, again we take time for discussion. We discover we have enacted emotion in motion. We have released tension related to important roles. Often we have faced something difficult. Sometimes we are exhilarated, sometimes tired. Nonetheless, the experience adds dimension to our personalities.

Another holistic class deals with our sensuality, that strong human quality so in need of validated avenues of expression. The class goes on a fantasy dance through air and water. I play the twenty-minute Side 1 of Mike Oldfield's *Hergest Ridge* and guide them through it. This fantasy may be danced with eyes open or closed.

The music begins quietly and I ask the women to regard themselves as strong, beautiful, powerful birds supported by air. As we progress I take them soaring, diving, and flowing. They have vast spaces of air and sky in which to move freely in every direction. They have the absolute support they need in their lives for their strong healthy bodies. They function perfectly. I remind them to feel the air about them and to remember it is connected to the whole universe, and so are they.

Then I guide them through a change, without stopping,

to a leaf floating softly through air with less purpose. Calmly they float down to water and the pleasant sensation of gliding down a river. They float passively from one spot to another, swirling and pausing. They feel the water and know its different kind of support. Sometimes the leaves are caught in an eddy or stopped by a rock. They pass on.

Another transition, and they are fish under the water. Once again they are purposeful and strong. They are sleek. They feel the under-water sensation. I bring them through many moves. (Every teacher may vary this fantasy.) Finally, they surface, not as fish but as women swimming nude. They must experience thoroughly the water on their bodies. They dip under and up. They bend and flow. They feel support and strength. Near the record's end they climb from a clear-water lake onto the hot sand where they lie on their backs, feel the sun, breathe deeply, and know their bodies.

Some would call therapeutic that dance which I name holistic. And rightly so. Of course there is a connection between therapy and dance. Therapy is the enacting of a specific activity — be it physical, mental, emotional, or spiritual — that enables one to know herself. Dancing qualifies as such an activity, whether one performs it alone or with others. I have friends who go dancing weekly at least, boastful and satisfied that by so doing they eliminate the necessity for psychological counseling.

I believe a college teacher of mine had an idea related to this counseling thought when she required us to write in a diary after each dance class. Here are excerpts from my "Journal of Improvisation Dance Class."

October 9, 1974   First dance session of this quarter. Did a thing with Pam — she using elbows, I, arms. Difficult but at one point there was a feeling of completeness for me, oblivious to everything, like when I dance alone at home. Only this was with another person. This new to me.

October 12

Upset today. Broke down in class. Teacher told class to do improvisation on this. Low-key, of each one's own feelings. I did floor writhings, gutteral sounds coming from deep within me. People didn't interact with each other. Not ready for this yet.

October 16

Three of us did improv. to weird instrumental sounds. *It felt good to be part of the group energy.*

October 26

Communication with others through movement delightful as opposed to usual verbal way. Perhaps more honest, our bodies not as experienced as our words in camouflaging our feelings.

October 31

The main problem for me in movement is "doing my own thing" versus "relating to others."

November 4

Saw an Improvisation performance by J. N. in San Francisco. Learned a lot. She's so free I felt intimidated. She had people from the audience join her and I was afraid she'd choose me. Glad she didn't. Will see her again next month to see if I've grown.

* * *

Whether it be called therapeutic or holistic, movement of the type described in this Holistic section is most successful when it provides a dancer the means for letting go. When one is able to release through dance she may attain wholeness of being. For energy discharged to the universe always is returned, as symbolized by the circle. When we admit dance to our lives we acquire that eternal tool with which we make our lives whole.

. . . to dance is to be whole is to dance is to be whole is to dance . . .

DANCE YOGA-CIZE

Dance Yoga-Cize is a course that brings together three movement disciplines: *exercises to music, isolated dancing, and yoga*. It is advertised as a class for people who love to dance and who want to exercise. It is designed to build personal strength, endurance, balance, and grace.

The idea for this course came to me as I noticed the many kinds of physical activities we women pursue for different reasons. We jog for endurance, we do slimming exercises for weight reduction, we even lift weights now for strength, we perform yoga for flexibility, and we take dance classes when we crave creative endeavor. Furthermore, most physically active women do more than one type of workout. The idea of a class that presented the perfect blend of several fitness activities seemed sensible.

So I chose those activities related to dance that would complement one another best and planned the class format as follows: *warmup, build-up, sustained activity* (mostly vibrant, with exceptions in the "slow and easy" version of the class, discussed later), *slow down, cool down, relaxation meditation.*

Generally, the *warmup* and *build-up* consist of leg stretches preceding three or four minutes of jogging and a short stretch dance. (The stretch dance is described elsewhere in the book.) Next come the exercises and the isolated dancing which together comprise the *sustained activity*. Sometimes, in conjunction with the isolated dancing, I include a full-body improvisational dance. We *slow down* and *cool down* with yoga. At the end, lying on our backs, we perform guided *relaxation meditation*. The music I use is rock, jazz, blues, and, for the exercises, something I call "pop disco-beat" because the rhythm is so pronounced.*

It is not my intention here to describe any of the exercises. All teachers and other women have favorite warmup routines that work every part of the body. Each teacher and every woman dancing alone at home will compose her own set to meet her individual needs and desires. After the standing and floor exercises we do leg lifts. This is the "modified" barre work, as we use chairs or even the wall when a barre is not available. A complete barre routine does not interest me. The only reason I use the barre at all is that the most strengthening exercises are those that defy gravity. In this vein the barre is perfect for leg lifts. (Actually, there is a current theory in teaching that use of the barre may be detrimental to achieving good balance. In his article, "The Barre — Aid or Crutch?", in the March, 1981 issue of Dancemagazine, Norman Thomson, a ballet dancer and teacher, says, ". . . dancing requires having the weight forward. Holding the barre gives an illusion of moving properly while the weight is really too far back.")

Finally, without holding on to anything, we perform plie routines to slow music, attending to their proper execution. The rib cage should be closed, the back straight not arched. The legs must be turned out to the degree only that allows the knees to bend in a vertical line above the

---

*   See Music Index for music used in Dance Yoga-Cize classes.

feet. Finally, heels must press into the floor upon the dancer's rising. I find plies to be important not only for strengthening legs but for improving balance and centering, concentration and poise — qualities useful aside from dance.

Sometimes students ask for therapeutic exercises for specific ailments. When this happens I stress the fact that I am a movement specialist not a physical therapist. If one has a particular problem she must seek help in other places. As in holistic medicine, my holistic approach to dance requires using preventive rather than corrective means — that is, exercises for healthy bodies.

Noone but the woman herself knows how her body feels. And in this class she is encouraged to develop a greater knowledge of her body by feeling it more intensely. She must trust her instincts to know how her body should move and, indeed, trust her body to tell her things about itself that she heretofore allowed only her mind to dictate. She may never have done these things before.

In Dance Yoga-Cize the women are encouraged to take back some of the power over the functioning of their bodies that they have given away to the "experts." Not every woman has activated her latent ability to heal herself but every person can assume the position of a thinking decision-maker in regard to her own body. We must stop following mindlessly the dictates of others, whether from doctors or dance teachers. But rather, we must weigh their suggestions, get other opinions, and do serious contemplation regarding what action we take. Mostly, we must tune into our perceptions about our bodies based on the historical and current knowledge of ourselves.

From the exercises we move into isolated dancing, the second part of the *sustained activity*. We form a circle, as always, and I guide the class through improvisational dancing with one body part at a time. The process is explained fully in other parts of *Power To The Dancers!* Isolated dancing performed in Dance Yoga-Cize affords the dancer the same benefits as it does in the Improvisational Rock and Creative Dance Workshops. It strengthens the body, increases flexibility, enhances body awareness, fosters concentration, nurtures improvisational skills, and builds movement confidence. Again the music is jazz-rock and the women are instructed to listen intently so they may respond to its subtleties.

Though teaching women to improvise in dancing is exciting and meaningful work, one must be aware that women taking a class like Dance Yoga-Cize do so mainly for the exercise. Though they like dance and expect it to be included in the course, for the most part they are not anxious to delve too deeply into the psychology of creating more spontaneous personal dances. *They want exercise* in the most satisfying and painless way they can get it. These "wants" must be given first priority and consideration in this class. What the women receive in addition to a firmer, stronger body — an introduction to improvisational movement via isolated dancing, an appreciation of the relatedness of differing exercise disciplines, and an awareness of the importance of equal mind-body functioning to produce a healthy, whole person — are bonuses not contracted for in their eyes. Teachers must realize this fact and conduct a Dance Yoga-Cize class accordingly.

The rhythm of the isolated dancing music is mostly medium to fast. The exception to this occurs in the "slow and easy" version of Dance Yoga-Cize. There are many women for whom the popular, vigorous dancercize and jazzercize classes are exhausting. Exercise should energize the person, not enervate her. Upon completing her dance class a woman may feel tired, but she should not feel debilitated. In the "slow and easy" version of Dance Yoga-Cize, the pace is slower than usual.* Both the exercises and the iso-

---

*   Music for "Slow and Easy" in Dance Yoga-Cize Music Index.

lated dancing are of a gentler kind. In the exercises we stretch more. In the dancing I play slow music. Older or less-active women love dance too and deserve to have as much dancing in their lives as do their younger and more able sisters. "Slow and easy" is designed for them especially.

Now we are two-thirds through a Dance Yoga-Cize class. A transition from dance to yoga takes place as I play *Music for Zen Meditation and Other Joys.* The women bring out their mats, sit on them and relax, breathe deeply and let themselves become quiet. We begin the *slow down* and *cool down.*

Yoga is an excellent discipline for promoting healthy mind-body functioning, for in the philosophy of yoga the individual is regarded as a unified whole. Mind, as well as body, is exercised. We breathe deeply and execute asanas (positions) for increased concentration, balance, energy, flexibility, and strength. There is no strain nor hurry involved, and each woman is in competition only with herself.

In our Western culture we perform many strenuous, demanding types of physical activities, including dance. Yoga complements such behavior. With its sustained, peaceful nature it counteracts the hectic character of dance exercises, treating the total rather than the fragmented person. For each individual posture is a complete experience in and of itself. Every asana begins precisely, with the body relaxed and in perfect position; the asana ends just as precisely. There are no short cuts, slighted movements, or sloppy endings. Energy through breathing is extended through the body to its boundary, the skin. As the women begin to know their bodies better through yoga, they become aware of this extended energy and learn how to use it to function efficiently.

The purpose of this book is not served by describing the yoga asanas. There are many good teachers, books, and television programs devoted exclusively to the practice of yoga. I recommend these to the reader. Often I suggest a supplemental yoga program for my students as well. I advise them that I, too, consider myself a student of yoga. Together we note our progress. Also, I emphasize no other kind of yoga but Hatha, which is physical yoga. Ha means sun and Tha means moon, referring to positive and negative life forces which are brought together and unified through postures and breathing exercises to form the perfect, whole self.

Something which *is* emphasized, however, is the similarity between postures and dance exercises, the goals of both being the same while the approach is different. As a yogi would say, the paths of self-realization all converge and blend, like diverse paths to the same mountaintop. For example, the Sun Salute, considered the perfect asana, involves several stages and the whole body working. It is similar in form and appearance to a series of dance exercises I call "side stretches" which, like the Sun Salute, strengthens the back, legs, and other parts through continual movements. As a woman learns to appreciate the similarity of goals of various movement programs, likewise she will begin to recognize the relationships between many aspects of her life. The more connections she perceives, the more unified her life becomes, until she is living holistically and in balance. Once in balance, or centered, she is in a position to accept that the universe is perfect, that behavior at any given moment fulfills a need, and that her life is, therefore, integrated into a unified whole or purpose.

Another emphasis in Dance Yoga-Cize is placed upon the elimination of stress. Stress is that condition in which the organism is squeezed, either mentally, emotionally, or physically. Today, classes are available for learning to recognize stress and its insidious affects upon our bodies. Yoga is the perfect counteraction to stress. In performing yoga we practice recognizing tightness, breathing deeply, and letting go of the tension. At the end of the yoga period each time we concentrate on how our bodies feel. The students must sense especially any tightness remaining in their faces. If they can feel a relaxed, calm forehead and no creases between the eyebrows, if the eyes seem wider open and the face generally smoother, they have consummated a yoga session that has freed them of stress.

We come now to the last part of a Dance Yoga-Cize class, the *relaxation meditation*. The students lie on their backs, covering themselves lightly if they wish and closing their eyes. There is no music. Sometimes I dim the lights before beginning the short guided visualization. Starting with feet, I make quiet, positive statements. "Your feet are peaceful and relaxed. All the small bones, the arch, and the ankle are at rest." I move up the body making suggestions to each part. "Let your hips become heavy; let them sink into the floor. Your stomach is calm; you completely let go." During the five-minute meditation, body tension disappears. At the end I say, "Now wiggle your fingers and toes." Then, quietly I add, "Turn to your left side and draw up your knees. When you are ready, open your eyes and sit up slowly."

It is time for the women to leave. My parting suggestion is that they allow their increased energy and peace of mind to carry them flowingly from the Dance Yoga-Cize class into and through the rest of their week.

MUSIC INDEX

IMPROVISATIONAL ROCK DANCE WORKSHOPS
CREATIVE DANCE WORKSHOPS
DANCE YOGA-CIZE

IMPROVISATIONAL ROCK WORKSHOP I

Lesson 1   *The Doors*, gold record album Elektra EKS
74007, 1967
The Butterfield Blues Band, *East West*, Elektra
EKL 315, 1966
Cream, *Disraeli Gears*, Atco Records (Atlantic)
SD 33-232, 1967
Bernard Krainis, *The Virtuoso Recorder*,
Odyssey Records 32 160144
Fleetwood Mac, *Kiln House*, Warner Bros.
Records

Lesson 2   *Russian Folk Instrumental Music*, USSR Melo-
diya and Capitol Records DT 10491
Bernard Krainis, *The Virtuoso Recorder*,
Odyssey Records 32 150144
Marshall Tucker, *Take The Highway*

Lesson 3   *Chants and Danses de Russie*, Polydor, Gravure
Universelle
Mozart, *Symphony in G*, first movement, no
particular recording, second movement
Beethoven, *Sonata Pathetique*, no particular

recording recommended
Scriabin, random selections
The Butterfield Blues Band, *East West,* Elektra
Records EKL 315, 1966

Lesson 4   Santana, *Abraxas,* Columbia Records KC 30130
Robin Trower, *Bridge of Sighs*, Chrysalis
Records 1057

Lesson 5   *Drums of Africa,* music of Western Africa
Face of Africa, London International TW 91204
Michael Olatunji, *Drums of Passion*, Columbia
CL 1412
African music, random selections from:
   Ninth Son
   The Best of Miriam Makeba

Lesson 6   Herbie Mann, *Push Push*, Embryo Records
SD 532
Grateful Dead, *Mars Hotel*

IMPROVISATIONAL ROCK WORKSHOP II

Lesson 1   Pink Floyd, *Prism Album*, The Gramophone
Co. Ltd., 1973
Cream, *Disraeli Gears*, Atco Records SD
33-232, 1967
Grateful Dead, *American Beauty*, Warner Bros.
Records, 1970
   Side 1, Cut 2 "Friend of the Devil"
      Cut 3 "Sugar Magnolia"
      Cut 4 "Operator"
      Cut 5 "Candyman"

Lesson 2   Herbie Mann, *Push Push*, Embryo Records

SD 532
Paul Horn, *Inside*, Epic Records, 1968
Taj Mahal, *Recycling the Blues*, Columbia Records KC 31505, 1972
Joni Mitchell, *Miles of Aisles*, Elektra/Asylum/Nonesuch Records AB 202
Nilsson, *Schmilsson*, Victor LSP 4515, 1971
Marshall Tucker, *Take The Highway*

Lesson 3   *Chants and Danses de Russie*, Polydor, Gravure Universelle
Peter Frampton, *Camel*, A & M Records SP 4389

Lesson 4   The Beatles, *Sergeant Pepper's Lonely Hearts Club Band*, Capital Records, SMAS 2653
The Edgar Winter Group, *Shock Treatment*, Epic PE 32461, 1974
Christopher Parkening, *Parkening Plays Bach*, Angel Records S-36041
Ravi Shankar, *The Sounds of India*, Columbia CL 2496, CS 9296
Country Joe and the Fish, *C.J. Fish*, Vanguard VSD 6555, 1970

Lesson 5   Michael Olatunji, *Drums of Passion*, Columbia CL 1412
Peter Frampton, *Camel*, A & M Records SP 4389

Lesson 6   Herbie Mann, *Push Push*, Embryo Records SD 532
Peter Frampton, *Camel*, A & M Records SP 4389
Janis Joplin, *Kosmic Blues Band*, Columbia Records 9913
Cream, *Disraeli Gears*, Atco Records SD 33-

232, 1967
The Beatles, *Sergeant Pepper's Lonely Hearts Club Band*, Capitol SMAS 2653

IMPROVISATIONAL ROCK WORKSHOP III

Lesson 1   Jeff Beck, *Blow by Blow*, Epic Records PE 33409
Grateful Dead, *American Beauty*, Warner Bros. Records, 1970

Lesson 2   Pointer Sisters, "How Long", from LP *Steppin'*, ABC Blue Thumb Records, 1975
Janis Joplin, *Full Tilt Boogie Band*, Columbia Records

Lesson 3   *Chants and Danses de Russie*, Polydor, Gravure Universelle
See Workshop I Lesson 5 Index for complete African music list.
Port Said, Music of Middle East, Audio Fidelity Records, AFSD 5833
Sergio Mendes and Brazil '77, *Primal Roots*, A & M Records SP 4353
Janis Joplin, *Kosmic Blues Band*, Columbia Records 9913

Lesson 4   Otis Redding, *Love Man*, Atco SD 33-289
Sergio Mendes and Brazil '77, *Primal Roots*, A & M SP 4353
Creedence Clearwater, *Creedence Clearwater Revival*, Fantasy Records 8382

Lesson 5   The Butterfield Blues Band, *East West*, Elektra EKL 315

Quicksilver Messenger Service, *Shady Grove*,
Capital Records SKAO 391
Janis Joplin, *Cheap Thrills*, Columbia PC 9700
1950s Rock and Roll music, selection available
on loan from libraries.

Lesson 6   The Mamas and The Papas, *The Mamas and
The Papas Deliver*, Dunhill Records D 50014
Jefferson Airplane, *Surrealistic Pillow*, RCA
Victor LSP 3766
Hair, The American Tribal Love Rock Musical,
RCA Victor LSO 1150

IMPROVISATIONAL ROCK WORKSHOP IV

Lesson 1   Tim Weisberg, *Four*, A & M Records SP 3658,
1974
The Edgar Winter Group, *Shock Treatment*,
Epic PE 32461, 1974
Merl Saunders, *Fire Up*, Fantasy 9471

Lesson 2   Jeff Beck, *Blow by Blow*, Epic PE 33409
Chuck Mangione, *Chase the Clouds Away*,
A & M Records SP 4518
Santana, *Abraxas*, Columbia KC 30130
Curtis Mayfield, *Superfly*, Buddah Records
CRS 8014 ST

Lesson 3   Ralph MacDonald, *The Path*, Marlin Records
2210, 1978
Donna Summer, *Love to Love You Baby*,
Oasis Records, 1975

Lesson 4   Tim Weisberg, *The Tim Weisberg Band*,
United Artists UA 1a 773G, 1977

The Edgar Winter Group, *Shock Treatment*,
Epic PE 32461, 1974
Sergio Mendes and Brazil '77, *Primal Roots*,
A & M SP 4353

Lesson 5   Donald Byrd Band and Voices, *A New Perspective*, Blue Note 84124
John Lennon, *John Lennon/Plastic Ono Band*,
Apple SW 3372
Sergio Mendes and Brazil '77, *Primal Roots*,
A & M SP 4353

Lesson 6   Tim Weisberg, *Four*, A & M SP 3658, 1974
Elton John, *Yellow Brick Road*, MCA Records
2-10003
"The Ballad of Danny Bailey"
"Dirty Little Girl"
"All The Girls Love Alice"

CREATIVE DANCE WORKSHOPS

I Improvisation

Donald Byrd Band, *A New Perspective*, Blue
Note 84124
The Edgar Winter Group, *Shock Treatment*,
Epic PE 32461
Mike Oldfield, *Hergest Ridge*, Virgin Records
(Atlantic), 1974
Preservation Hall Jazz Band, *Sweet Emma*,
Preservation Hall Records, VPH/VPS-2
Joni Mitchell, *Don Juan's Reckless Daughter*,
Asylum Records BB701
Music for Zen Meditation and Other Joys,
Verve Records V6-8632

II The Physical Tools
    The Butterfield Blues Band, *East West*,
    Elecktra EKL-315
    B.J. Walberg, *Dance-a-long*, Folkways Records,
    FC 7651 A

III With Others
    John Lennon, *John Lennon/Plastic Ono Band*,
    Apple SW 3372
    Michael Olatunji, *Drums of Passion*, Columbia
    CL 1412
    Sergio Mendes and Brazil '77, *Primal Roots*,
    A & M SP 4353
    Paul Horn, *Inside*, Epic, 1968
    Ravi Shankar, *The Sounds of India*, Columbia
    CS 9296
    Belly Dance Navel Academy, P.J. Records
    LPS-30
    Port Said, Audio Fidelity AFSD 5833
    Chants and Danses de Russie, Polydor Gravure
    Universelle
    Russian Folk Instrumental Music, Capitol DT
    10491 & SSR Melodiya
    Music for Zen Meditation and Other Joys,
    Verve V6-8634

IV Sounds
    Totentanz (Dance of Death), a dance stage pro-
    duction by Carlos Carvajal of Dance Spectrum
    Co. of San Francisco. Recorded in Canada.
    Erik Satie, *The Electronic Spirit of Erik Satie*,
    London 18066

V Interpretations
    Misa Criolla, The Catholic Mass based on
    rhythms of Hispanic America, Monitor Records

MFS 753

Camel, *The Snow Goose*, Janus Records JKS 7016

Chuck Mangione, *Children of Sanchez*, A & M Records, 1978

VI Holistic

Tchaikovsky, *Pathetique Symphony*, first movement

Rimsky-Korsakov, *Schaherazade,* first movement

Erik Satie, *The Velvet Gentleman*, London DES 18036, "Trois Gymnopedies"

Christopher Parkening, *Parkening Plays Bach*, Angel S-36041

B.J. Walberg, *Dance-a-long*, Folkways Records FC 7651 A

Tchaikovsky, *The Nutcracker Suite*, Columbia LP 51025, "Arabian Dance"

Donald Byrd Band, *A New Perspective*, Blue Note Records 84124, "Cristo Retentor"

Mike Oldfield, *Hergest Ridge*, Virgin Records (Atlantic), 1974

DANCE YOGA-CIZE

Warmup and Build-up (Jog and Stretch)

Sergio Mendes and Brazil '77, *Primal Roots*, A & M Records SP 4353, "Pomba Gira" (jog)

Weather Report, *Heavy Weather*, Columbia Records 34418, 1977, "Birdland" (jog)

Donald Byrd Band, *A New Perspective*, Blue Note 84124, "Cristo Retentor" (stretch and plies)

Sustained Activity (Exercises and Isolated Dancing)
> Van McCoy, *Lonely Dancer*, MCA Records
> 3071, "Lonely Dancer", "The Samba" (exer-
> cises)
> The Crusaders, *Rhapsody and Blues*, MCA
> Records 5124 "Honky Tonk Struttin' "
> (exercises)
> Ralph MacDonald, *The Path*, Marlin Records
> 2210, 1978 (isolated dancing)
> Carly Simon, *The Best of Carly Simon*, Eleck-
> tra Records 7E 1048B, "Attitude Dancing",
> "Mockingbird" (isolated dancing)
> *Blood, Sweat & Tears*, Columbia CS 9720
> (isolated dancing)
> Alice Coltrane, *Eternity*, Warner Bros. Records
> BS 2916, "Los Caballos" (isolated dancing)
> B.B. King, *The Best of B.B. King*, ABC Records
> X-767, 1973 (isolated dancing)
> Flora Purim, *What's That She Said*, Fantasy
> Records M-9081, 1978 (isolated dancing)

Slow Down and Cool Down (Yoga and Relaxation Meditation)
> Steven Halpern, *Spectrum Suite*, Halpern
> Sounds Records 770 Stereo, 1977
> Larkin, *Ocean* (oh-see-on), Wind Sung Sounds,
> Stanford, 1979 (flute and whale music)
> *Music for Zen Meditation and Other Joys*,
> Verve Records V6-8634
> Robert Schroder, *Floating Music*, IC Klaus
> Schulze Prod., 1980 KS 80.001, Germany

Slow and Easy Version of Dance Yoga-Cize
> Boz Scaggs, *Slow Dancer*, Columbia Records
> IC 32760
> John Klemmer, *Touch*, ABC Records 922

The Crusaders, *Rhapsody and Blues,* MCA
Records 5124
The Best of Isaac Hayes, Enterprise Records
ENS 7510
Roberta Flack, *First Take,* Atlantic Records
SD 8230
Chuck Mangione, *Chase The Clouds Away,*
A & M Records SP 4518
Don Ellis, *Haiku,* Objective Music Co. MPS
BASF MB 25341

A NOTE ON THE MUSIC LIST

The music I use in my Workshops comes mostly from the 1960s and 1970s, with the exception of the ethnic and the "old" classical music mentioned. I continue to use this same list for good reason. In the psychedelic era music opened us up like flowers. For me, great growth came with dance in that period. So, as my teaching career is an integral part of my personal growth and as the historical 60s affected us all so profoundly, this list is a valuable resource of "new" classics that accompanied abundant individual and social change in its time. Furthermore, in naming titles, my purpose is not necessarily to educate the reader musically but, rather, to illustrate that a wide variety of music should be used.

That is not to say, of course, I do not advocate dancing to later music as well, in the areas of soft, hard, and punk rock; "space" music like that of Kitaro, Robert Schroder, and Andreas Vollenweider; and innovative jazz by George Winston, James Newton, and Barbara Higbie, to mention only a few. Nor do I ignore folk music, heavy metal, or pop vocals by Tina Turner, Cyndi Lauper, Bruce Springsteen, and Madonna, for example. I move to all sounds. And I encourage teachers and others to do the same, drawing from my classics list, as well as creatively choosing their own favorites for accompaniment to joyful dancing.

"The world doesn't need any more guru types and I don't want to come off sounding like one, so don't quote me, but it seems to me that we humans are all striving towards the same purpose. Not that I know what it is, mind you. Nobody does. We just keep at it, and all of us have a different way of getting there. I figure when we feel good, we're getting close. The one thing I do know for sure is that dancing makes me feel very good, so I must be going in the right direction by doing it."

From one ordinary dancing woman who is a friend of mine and would like to leave her name unsigned.

Metamorphous Press

METAMORPHOUS PRESS is a publisher and distributor of books and other media providing resources for personal growth and positive changes. MPI publishes and distributes leading edge ideas that help people strengthen their unique talents and discover that we all create our own realities.

Many of our titles have centered around NeuroLinguistic Programming (NLP). NLP is an exciting, practical and powerful model of human behavior and communication that has been able to connect observable patterns of behavior and communication to the processes that underlie them.

METAMORPHOUS PRESS provides selections in many subject areas such as communication, health and fitness, education, business and sales, therapy, selections for young persons, and other subjects of general and specific interest. Our products are available in fine bookstores around the world. Among our Distributors for North America are:

Baker & Taylor	The Distributors
Bookpeople	Inland Book Co.
New Leaf Distributors	Starlite Distributors
Pacific Pipeline	Moving Books, Inc.

For those of you overseas, we are distributed by:
Airlift (UK, Western Europe)
Bewitched Books (Victoria, Australia)

New selections are added regularly and the availability and prices change so ask for a current catalog or to be put on our mailing list. If you have difficulty finding our products in your favorite store or if you prefer to order by mail we will be happy to make our books and other products available to you directly.

YOUR INVOLVEMENT WITH WHAT WE DO AND YOUR INTEREST IS ALWAYS WELCOME — please write to us at:

Metamorphous Press, Inc.
3249 N.W. 29th Avenue
P.O. Box 10616
Portland, Oregon 97210
(503) 228-4972

HEALTH AND FITNESS BOOKS
from Metamorphous Press, Inc.

Quantity

☐ The Power of Balance
A Rolfing View of Health
Brian W. Fahey, Ph.D.

This is a book about the importance of balance in all aspects of life. It expands upon the original ideas about improving health by balancing body structure first developed by Ida P. Rolf, Ph.D. Dr. Rolf developed a system of direct body manipulation and education known as Structural Integration, or "Rolfing." The Rolfing process educates, reorganizes, and balances the body into an integrated system. The balance achieved from Rolfing works its way through the whole system to improve our level of health. Rolfing ideas can be applied to all aspects of daily life, including how we sit, stand, walk, do our jobs, play, and ultimately, how we feel about ourselves. Reading this book can be a step toward achieving a high level of structural balance, energy, and well-being for yourself.
0-943920-52-3. . . . . Hardcover $19.95

☐ Power To The Dancers!
Beverly Kalinin

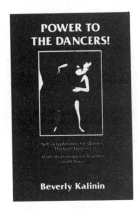

Power To The Dancers! is about the relationship between personal growth and dancing. Infinitely more than an exercise book, **Power To The Dancers!** adds dimensions to fitness by addressing the whole person. Author and teacher Beverly Kalinin shows how she discovered dancing to be the guide on her life journey and encourages others to do the same. Personal in nature, universal in appeal, the book is a chronological series of essays, poems, anecdotes, dreams, and observations on teaching dance, as well as detailed workshops on Improvisational Rock Dancing, Creative Dance, and Dance Yoga-Cize. The mood of this book is inspirational as well as instructive.
0-943920-44-2. . . . . Softcover $14.95

☐ Your Balancing Act
Discovering New Life Through
Five Dimensions of Wellness
Carolyn J. Taylor, R.N.

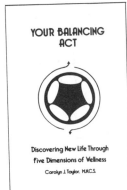

This intriguing new book in the field of Neuro-Linguistic Programming presents the systematic exercises and new material for changing the all important beliefs that underly the conditions that lead to wellness. Health, relationships, creativity, happiness and personal success are just some of the aspects of our lives that are effected by our beliefs, says Taylor. Recognizing that beliefs are a very powerful force in our behavior is the beginning of a process that can help us to create positive and productive results in virtually every capacity of life. Presented in an easily read and understood format, this book is a must for anyone who cares about their health or the quality of their life.
0-943920-75-2. . . . . Softcover $12.95

Quantity

☐ Fitness Without Stress
A Guide to The Alexander Technique
Robert M. Rickover

The Alexander Technique is today recognized to be one of the most sophisticated and powerful methods of personal transformation available. It has a long history of helping people improve their posture and co-ordination and it has proven to be an extraordinarily effective way to relieve stress-related conditions such as backache, depression, migraine, asthma and TMJ disorders. This fascinating method of achieving psychophysical well-being is fully described in this new book that can be enjoyed by readers with no previous experience as well as those who have already had lessons.
0-943920-32-9. . . . . Hardcover $14.95

FITNESS WITHOUT STRESS

A GUIDE TO
THE ALEXANDER TECHNIQUE

by Robert M. Rickover

☐ The Elusive Obvious
Moshe Feldenkrais

In both his individual, hands-on body work (Functional Integration) and his group classes (Awareness in Movement) the author guides clients to discover for themselves what normal or optimum movement feels like. This sensing will then reprogram – his term is "rewire" – the brain accordingly.
0-916990-09-5. . . . . . . Hardcover $19.95

☐ The Master Moves
Moshe Feldenkrais

All Moshe's major ideas on movement, human development, sensitivity, awareness, and so forth are presented both as expositions and explorations through movement lessons. These lessons, part of his unique contribution to human development, are the key to understanding the Feldenkrais method. Use this book well and you will be surprised at the results.
0-916990-15-X . . . . . Hardcover $14.95

☐ Turn Your Pressure Valve Down
Richard Flint

Pressure demands understanding in order to turn it into a creative force. This book is designed to help with that understanding. It deals in practical realities with: understanding the value of pressure to your life; how pressure works in the human life; how pressure gains control of your life; and how to turn pressure into productive growth. It's more than just another book on stress management – it's a recipe filled with ingredients to make pressure the productive growth tool it was meant to be.
9-937851-22-1. . . . . . Softcover $10.00